ADB CLIENT PERCEPTIONS SURVEY 2020

MULTINATIONAL SURVEY OF STAKEHOLDERS

OCTOBER 2021

ADB

ASIAN DEVELOPMENT BANK

© 2021 Asian Development Bank
6 ADB Avenue, Mandaluyong City, 1550 Metro Manila, Philippines
Tel +63 2 8632 4444; Fax +63 2 8636 2444
www.adb.org

Some rights reserved. Published in 2021.

ISBN 978-92-9269-087-8 (print); 978-92-9269-088-5 (electronic); 978-92-9269-089-2 (ebook)
Publication Stock No. TCS210302-2
DOI: http://dx.doi.org/10.22617/TCS210302-2

Notes:
In this publication, "$" refers to United States dollars.

Cover design by Josef Ilumin.

Contents

Tables and Figures

Tables

Figures

Foreword

Consultation, engagement, and collaboration serve as the backbone of many approaches designed to tackle the most entrenched issues facing the world today. Consulting with clients and stakeholders and encouraging them to uphold their interests and areas of expertise can give an organization a broader and more meaningful perspective, improve its understanding of issues within a sector or a country, and build consensus to define good practice. The long-term success of an organization is closely linked to its ability to identify and meet client needs, and adapt to their changing requirements and expectations. Client satisfaction, for most organizations, is a vital goal. The Asian Development Bank (ADB) must therefore consult and engage with its clients, to fulfill its mission of helping its developing member countries (DMC) reduce poverty and give their citizens a better quality of life.

ADB works with various clients, including central and local government agencies, the private sector, civil society organizations, academia, think tanks, individual researchers, and the media, and collaborates and synergizes with multilateral and bilateral development partners. ADB strives to build long-term relationships of trust with its diverse stakeholders and regularly engages in dialogue with its clients. These tasks have become more challenging amid the coronavirus disease (COVID-19) pandemic and with inequality in the spotlight, as organizations must deal with significant shifts in client expectations. Soliciting timely feedback from clients is thus critical, to better inform ADB's strategies and operations, especially in such difficult times.

ADB's Strategy 2030 recognizes the "increasingly diversified and sophisticated" needs of clients and commits ADB to "[customizing] its approach to meet the varying needs of its diverse client base" and also to "[supporting] innovative financial products and [facilitating] a culture of innovation and responsiveness to changing client needs." This spirit is fully reflected in the Strategy 2030–aligned corporate results framework (CRF), which includes a CRF indicator that measures client satisfaction with the use of ADB's knowledge products and services, as well as three tracking indicators that gauge client satisfaction with ADB's development effectiveness, responsiveness, and collaboration with development partners.

Recognizing the challenges in its path, and the importance of determining how it can collaborate and connect more effectively with its clients, ADB commissioned a public opinion research consultancy firm to conduct a robust client engagement exercise in order to identify key issues of importance on an arm's-length basis, to ensure objectivity and credibility of the results, and to collect data for the new CRF indicators. The survey also presented an opportunity to obtain information not captured through other existing forms of client outreach.

The survey covered a wide range of ADB clients in more than 40 countries in Asia and the Pacific, and more than 20 countries in other regions, and gathered valuable feedback from more than 1,200 clients.

This publication discusses noteworthy points brought out during the survey. It is hoped that this report will help its users understand the needs of ADB's DMC clients and assess the extent to which ADB is meeting those needs, further improve ADB's interaction with its clients and partners, and bring a more equitable and sustainable future within closer reach.

Bambang Susantono
Vice-President for Knowledge Management and Sustainable Development

Summary and Key Findings

SURVEY HIGHLIGHTS

- High level of familiarity with the Asian Development Bank (ADB) among clients

- Room for ADB to increase awareness and familiarity among Primary Clients in the private sector

- Overall usefulness of ADB knowledge products and services (KPS) and knowledge-centered events, particularly in policy, program, and project design, preparation, and implementation

- Room to heighten clients' satisfaction with ADB's responsiveness, development effectiveness, and collaboration with development partners

- Positive impact of ADB's response to the coronavirus disease (COVID-19) pandemic

- Promotion of the use of e-learning courses and self-education materials of the Asian Development Bank Institute (ADBI)

- Room to increase client familiarity with ADB's evaluation KPS and encourage their use

The vast majority of clients of the Asian Development Bank (ADB) claim at least some knowledge of ADB and its activities.

High familiarity with ADB in general, but relatively lower familiarity among Primary Clients in the private sector. Familiarity with ADB is high among clients, particularly among Primary Clients, 90% of which say they are "very" or "somewhat" knowledgeable about ADB and its activities, versus 87% of all respondents. This high level of familiarity is driven by clients from East Asia (98%) and Central and West Asia (95%).

The lowest level of familiarity, on the other hand, is recorded among Primary Clients in the private sector, where about one in four (26%) are "not too knowledgeable" about ADB. The ratings and satisfaction of clients and Primary Clients in the private sector are generally lower than those of clients

in government. The disparity leaves room for ADB to increase awareness of and familiarity with ADB among its Primary Clients in the private sector.

Overall perception of usefulness of ADB knowledge products and services (KPS), but with disparities in their level of use. A positive trend is observed for the corporate results framework (CRF) indicator "usefulness of ADB's knowledge products, services, and events." Three in four clients surveyed say that they are familiar with ADB KPS and knowledge-centered events, and overall, a similar proportion find these highly useful. From 3.89 in 2019, this CRF indicator rose to 3.96 in 2020, among all respondents. The indicator for Primary Clients in 2020 was significantly higher than the indicator for all respondents in 2019. Primary Clients consider ADB KPS most useful in designing, preparing, and implementing policies and programs, as well as in developing learning materials.

At the product level, the KPS are perceived as very useful, but there are disparities in their level of use. Webinars, seminars, workshops, and conferences are all used efficiently and to a high degree by a majority of ADB clients and are considered highly useful. Capacity building / Training is common practice among Primary Clients and is viewed as the most useful among all ADB KPS. Other KPS, including policy dialogue and related activities, are much less widely used.

Advocating greater use of these products among clients and showcasing their usefulness in clients' work can expand product reach. The 2020 increase in the "usefulness of ADB KPS" indicator (compared with the previous year) among all respondents is an encouraging sign.

To strengthen awareness of ADB's KPS and of the type of support that ADB can provide to clients in the private sector, ADB can develop materials specifically suited to clients' needs; showcase the broad range of ADB knowledge products available; and give clients stronger guidance in using the new knowledge efficiently in their work.

Room to heighten clients' satisfaction with ADB's responsiveness, development effectiveness, and collaboration with development partners. There are differences in ratings among the four CRF indicators. "Usefulness of ADB's KPS" is rated relatively high (78% of all respondents and 81% of Primary Clients rate ADB KPS "extremely" or "very" useful). But "ADB's responsiveness" and "ADB's collaboration with development partners" have a slightly lower rating (only about 63% of Primary Clients are "extremely" or "very" satisfied with these).

Also, while ADB's development effectiveness gets a slightly higher satisfaction rating, at 75%, this rating is perceived to have declined from 88% in 2012. Although the development context has dramatically changed and development challenges are now much more complex, this perception among developing member countries (DMCs) is worthwhile investigating further, to ensure that ADB's efforts keep pace with the evolving development needs of its DMC members.

Inadequate responsiveness and excessive bureaucracy are concerns raised by clients to explain some of the negative overall satisfaction ratings of ADB's responsiveness. The context of, and reasons behind, these concerns are worth identifying, to show ADB's willingness to adapt to meet client expectations. Demonstrating ADB's responsiveness and development effectiveness is important, in order to avoid any negative effects on overall satisfaction with ADB support at the country level.

The low level of satisfaction with ADB's collaboration with development partners demands a prompt and suitable response as well from ADB. Given the increasingly difficult development setting and the scarcity of resources, clients depend highly on close coordination and enhanced collaboration among development partners to optimize development impact.

Positive impact of ADB's response to the coronavirus disease (COVID-19) pandemic. About two-thirds of the Primary Clients surveyed claim some familiarity with ADB's response to the coronavirus disease (COVID-19) pandemic (63% are "very" or "moderately" familiar). The vast majority of Primary Clients surveyed agree that ADB support in dealing with COVID-19 has had some positive impact on their country.

Among the Primary Clients familiar with ADB's COVID-19 response, 80% rate the speed of response "good" or "excellent," and 81% believe that ADB tailors its response to the country context. The size of ADB's response in relation to the country's needs and the KPS support provided are also perceived as "excellent" or "good" by a majority of Primary Clients (76% and 79%, respectively).

Promotion of the use of Asian Development Bank Institute (ADBI) e-learning courses and self-education materials. ADBI KPS are seen as relevant to the main work activities and tasks of the respondents, particularly the design and implementation of new policies, programs, or projects.

Self-education is also regarded by respondents as a relatively important activity in their work, highlighting the potential for ADBI assistance in learning and knowledge development. However, ADBI KPS are deemed slightly less relevant to this task. Demonstrating the range of ADBI products that can help clients develop and enrich their knowledge will address this perception.

Room to increase client familiarity with ADB's evaluation KPS and encourage their use. The level of familiarity with these products and services is relatively low among ADB clients: only a third of clients surveyed say they are "very" or "moderately" familiar with ADB's evaluation KPS.

But among clients familiar with these products and services, the vast majority find ADB's evaluation KPS "extremely," "very," or "somewhat" useful. This suggests that there is potential for increasing their effective use.

Abbreviations

ADB   Asian Development Bank

ADBI   Asian Development Bank Institute

COVID-19   coronavirus disease

CRF   corporate results framework

CSO   civil society organization

DMC   developing member country

FCAS   fragile and conflict-affected state(s)

HIC   high-income country

KPS   knowledge products and services

LIC   low-income country

LMIC   lower middle-income country

SIDS   small island developing state(s)

UMIC   upper middle-income country

1 Introduction

Background and Objectives

Strategy 2030[1] of the Asian Development Bank (ADB) recognizes the "increasingly diversified and sophisticated" needs of clients and commits ADB to "[customizing] its approach to meet the varying needs of its diverse client base" and "[supporting] innovative financial products and [facilitating] a culture of innovation and responsiveness to changing client needs."

The ADB corporate results framework (CRF),[2] aligned with Strategy 2030, includes the following:

- a results framework indicator that measures client satisfaction with the use of ADB's knowledge products; and
- three tracking indicators measuring client satisfaction with ADB's development effectiveness, responsiveness, and collaboration with development partners.

To collect data for these new CRF indicators and to find out whether ADB is meeting its clients' needs, GlobeScan[3] conducted this 2020 Client Perceptions Survey. The survey also presented an opportunity to obtain information not captured through other existing forms of client outreach for ADB.

To better understand the increasingly diversified and sophisticated needs of ADB clients through a wide-ranged client perceptions survey.

Geographic Coverage

The survey covered a wide range of ADB clients in more than 40 countries in Asia and the Pacific, and more than 20 countries in other regions. The respondents came from government, civil society organizations (CSOs), the private/business sector, media, and universities, think tanks, and academia. Individual researchers and other organizations were also represented.

Note: Percentage figures in this report may not add up to 100% because of rounding.

---

[1] ADB. 2018. *Strategy 2030: Achieving a Prosperous, Inclusive, Resilient, and Sustainable Asia and the Pacific.* Manila.
[2] ADB. 2019. *ADB Corporate Results Framework, 2019–2024.* Manila.
[3] GlobeScan Incorporated is a global stakeholder and reputation research consultancy firm headquartered in Canada. The company, founded in 1987, has a network of research partners in more than 70 countries and subscribes to the standards of the World Association of Opinion and Marketing Research Professionals (ESOMAR). GlobeScan also conducted the ADB Client Perceptions Surveys in 2009 and 2012.

2 Survey Respondents

Respondent Profile and Definitions

ADB Respondents

In this report, the term "ADB respondents" or "ADB clients" refers to survey respondents that say they are "not too," "somewhat," or "very" knowledgeable about ADB and its activities (screening criteria applied in question S2a; see Appendix 2).

These respondents were recruited from among the entities listed in the main ADB database of clients.

Primary Clients

The term "Primary Clients" is used in this report to refer mostly to government agencies and private sector entities in ADB developing member countries (DMCs) that have taken part in ADB-financed operations.

Academic and research institutions and think tanks that are mainly Asian Development Bank Institute (ADBI) respondents are regarded as non-Primary Clients for non-ADBI-related

questions. Government clients are further classified into three groups, as follows:

- Government 1: Prime minister's / President's office, and ministries of finance, economy, and development planning, as well as parliament/legislature;
- Government 2: Other ministries/departments (transport, energy, agriculture, health, education, industry and trade, etc.); and
- Government 3: Regional, provincial, and municipal governments.

Composition

Of the 6,560 ADB clients that were successfully invited to take part in the 2020 ADB Client Perceptions Survey (their contact details were accurate), 1,054 completed the survey, and 162 submitted a partial response. The total end sample therefore comprises 1,216 respondents that completed or responded partially to the survey. Among these respondents, 582 were identified as Primary Clients. A further breakdown of respondents is shown in Tables 1–3, and Figures 1 and 2.

Table 1: All Respondents, by Subregion

Subregion	No. of Invitations Sent	No. of Completed Interviews	Response Rate (%)
Central and West Asia	452	100	22.10
East Asia	459	73	15.90
Pacific	174	41	23.60
South Asia	962	177	18.40
Southeast Asia	3,150	581	18.40
Other	1,363	82	6.00
Total (completed interviews)	**6,560**	**1,054**	**16.10**
Total (completed + partial interviews)	**6,560**	**1,216**	**18.50**

Note: "Other" pertains to respondents outside the listed group.
Source: Asian Development Bank Client Perceptions Survey 2020.

Table 2: Primary Client Respondents, by Subregion

Subregion	No. of Invitations Sent	No. of Completed Interviews	Response Rate (%)
Central and West Asia	377	75	19.90
East Asia	321	46	14.30
Pacific	130	31	23.80
South Asia	484	91	18.80
Southeast Asia	1,469	257	17.50
Other	32	4	12.50
Total (completed interviews)	**2,813**	**504**	**17.90**
Total (completed + partial interviews)	**2,813**	**582**	**20.70**

Note: "Other" pertains to respondents outside the listed group.
Source: Asian Development Bank Client Perceptions Survey 2020.

Table 3: All Respondents, by Stakeholder Group

Sector	Total Sample	Primary Clients
Government 1 – Central: Prime Minister's / President's office; ministries of finance, economy, development planning; parliament/legislature	143	120
Government 2 – Line: Ministries/Departments (transport, energy, agriculture, health, education, industry and trade, etc.)	372	305
Government 3 – Local: Regional, provincial, and municipal governments	83	70
Civil society organizations: Nongovernment organizations, charitable and not-for-profit organizations	100	8
Private/Business sector	364	23
Media	14	1
Universities, think tanks, academia	239	8
Other	121	47
Total Respondents	**1,436**	**582**

Note: Private/Business sector clients are involved in sovereign projects, and therefore do not include clients of ADB's Private Sector Operations Department (PSOD), which take part in nonsovereign projects.
Source: Asian Development Bank Client Perceptions Survey 2020.

Figure 1: Demographic Profile of All Respondents
(%)

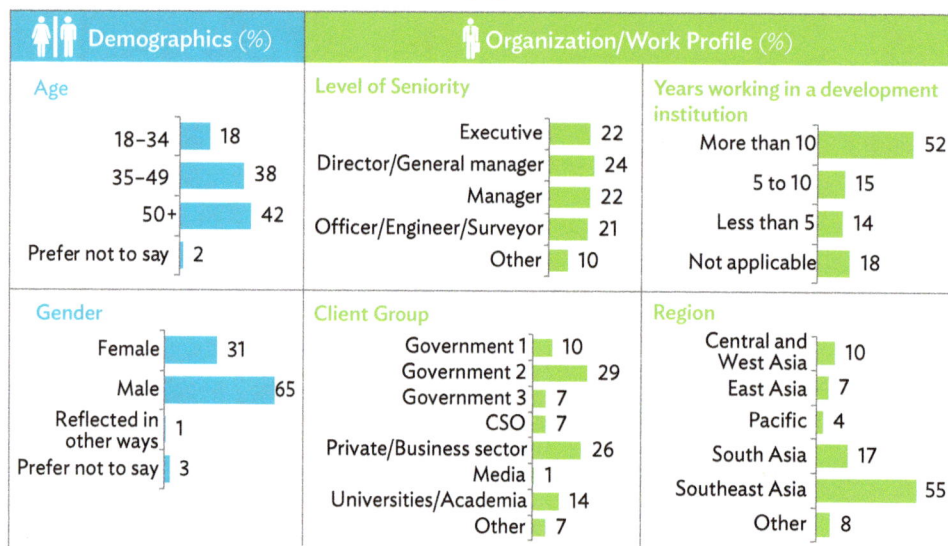

Demographics (%)	Organization/Work Profile (%)	
Age	**Level of Seniority**	**Years working in a development institution**
18–34 18	Executive 22	More than 10 52
35–49 38	Director/General manager 24	5 to 10 15
50+ 42	Manager 22	Less than 5 14
Prefer not to say 2	Officer/Engineer/Surveyor 21	Not applicable 18
	Other 10	
Gender	**Client Group**	**Region**
Female 31	Government 1 10	Central and West Asia 10
Male 65	Government 2 29	East Asia 7
Reflected in other ways 1	Government 3 7	Pacific 4
Prefer not to say 3	CSO 7	South Asia 17
	Private/Business sector 26	Southeast Asia 55
	Media 1	Other 8
	Universities/Academia 14	
	Other 7	

CSO = civil society organization; Government 1 = central government; Government 2 = line ministries; Government 3 = local governments.
Note: "Other" pertains to respondents outside the listed group.
Source: Asian Development Bank Client Perceptions Survey 2020.

Figure 2: Demographic Profile of Primary Client Respondents
(%)

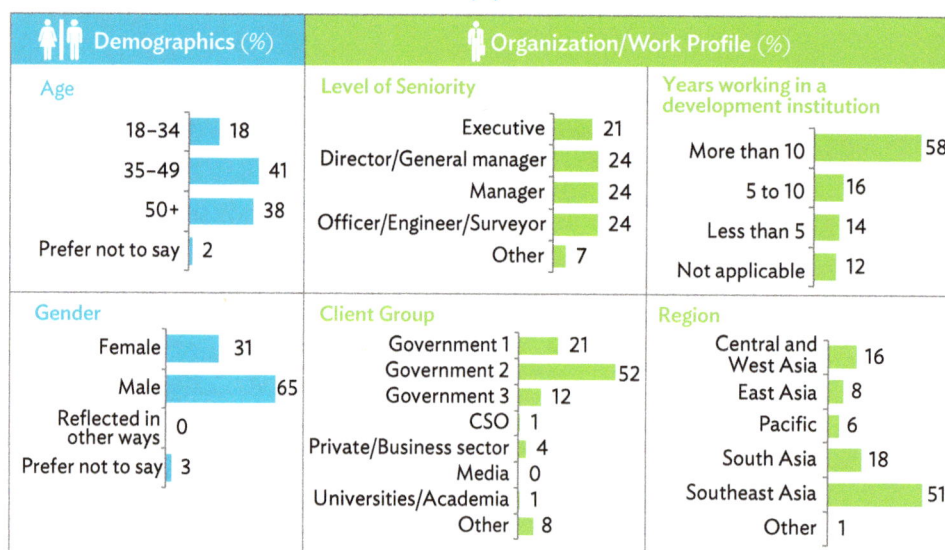

Demographics (%)	Organization/Work Profile (%)	
Age	**Level of Seniority**	**Years working in a development institution**
18–34 18	Executive 21	More than 10 58
35–49 41	Director/General manager 24	5 to 10 16
50+ 38	Manager 24	Less than 5 14
Prefer not to say 2	Officer/Engineer/Surveyor 24	Not applicable 12
	Other 7	
Gender	**Client Group**	**Region**
Female 31	Government 1 21	Central and West Asia 16
Male 65	Government 2 52	East Asia 8
Reflected in other ways 0	Government 3 12	Pacific 6
Prefer not to say 3	CSO 1	South Asia 18
	Private/Business sector 4	Southeast Asia 51
	Media 0	Other 1
	Universities/Academia 1	
	Other 8	

CSO = civil society organization; Government 1 = central government; Government 2 = line ministries; Government 3 = local governments.
Note: "Other" pertains to respondents outside the listed group.
Source: Asian Development Bank Client Perceptions Survey 2020.

Supplemental ADBI Survey

Besides the main ADB survey, a special supplemental survey using a different database supplied by ADBI was conducted. This survey had the following features:

- Screener questions posed to respondents pertained only to their contact section at ADBI and demographic information.

- Survey questions asked were worded in exactly the same way as those in the main ADB survey, in order for the data to be comparable and to allow both data sets to be merged.

- The methodology was the same as that used in the main ADB survey: a self-completion questionnaire answered online.

- The completed interviews in this supplemental ADBI survey totaled 220.

- All respondents from the ADBI database were categorized as non–Primary Clients.

Respondents familiar with ADBI were slightly more skewed toward those aged over 50, with a high level of seniority (occupying executive, director / general manager positions) and having more than 10 years of work experience with a development institution. The composition of respondents for the ADBI survey is shown in Table 4.

Table 4: Composition of Respondents for ADBI Survey

Survey Category	No. of Completed Interviews
Main ADB survey (with ADB database)	1,216
Short ADBI survey (with ADBI database)	220
Total completed ADBI interviews: ADBI respondents who either answered only ADBI-related questions or answered both ADB- and ADBI-related questions (merged ADB and ADBI databases)	1,009
Total completed ADB + ADBI interviews: All respondents (merged ADB and ADBI databases)	1,436

ADB = Asian Development Bank, ADBI = Asian Development Bank Institute.

Source: Asian Development Bank Client Perceptions Survey 2020.

Familiarity with ADB

All Respondents

The clients surveyed have a high level of familiarity with ADB overall (87% are "very" or "somewhat" knowledgeable about ADB and its activities), as shown in Figure 3.

This high familiarity is driven by clients from East Asia and Central and West Asia (98% and 95%, respectively, describe themselves as "very" or "somewhat" knowledgeable).

Clients in government organizations, particularly those in the Government 3 group, are the most familiar with ADB (one in three say they are "very" knowledgeable).

Figure 3: Familiarity with ADB, All Respondents (%)

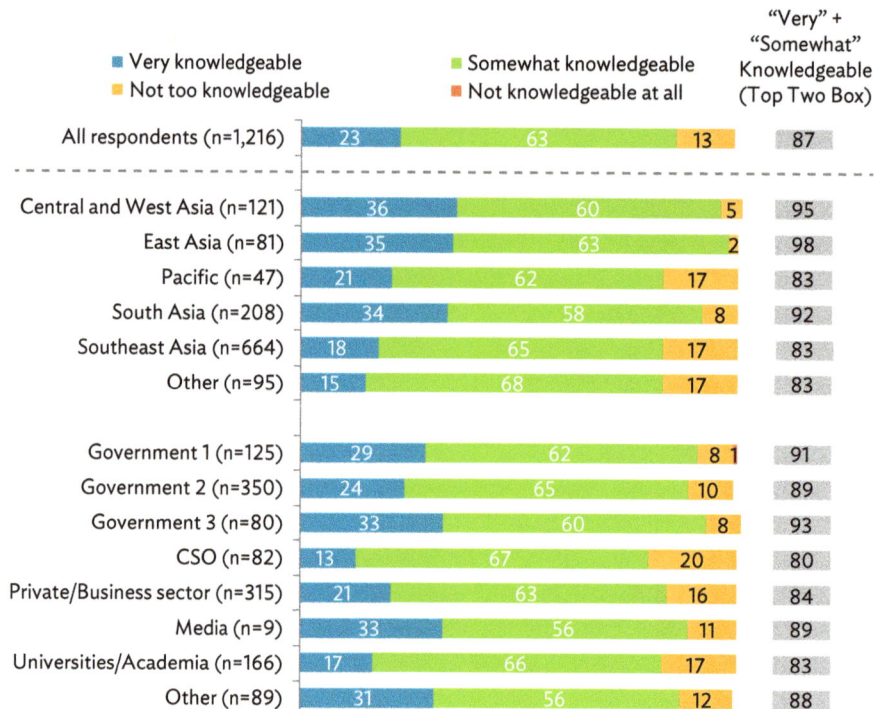

Legend:
- Very knowledgeable
- Somewhat knowledgeable
- Not too knowledgeable
- Not knowledgeable at all

Respondent group	Very knowledgeable	Somewhat knowledgeable	Not too knowledgeable	Not knowledgeable at all	"Very" + "Somewhat" Knowledgeable (Top Two Box)
All respondents (n=1,216)	23	63	13		87
Central and West Asia (n=121)	36	60	5		95
East Asia (n=81)	35	63	2		98
Pacific (n=47)	21	62	17		83
South Asia (n=208)	34	58	8		92
Southeast Asia (n=664)	18	65	17		83
Other (n=95)	15	68	17		83
Government 1 (n=125)	29	62	8	1	91
Government 2 (n=350)	24	65	10		89
Government 3 (n=80)	33	60	8		93
CSO (n=82)	13	67	20		80
Private/Business sector (n=315)	21	63	16		84
Media (n=9)	33	56	11		89
Universities/Academia (n=166)	17	66	17		83
Other (n=89)	31	56	12		88

ADB = Asian Development Bank, CSO = civil society organization, Government 1 = central government, Government 2 = line ministries, Government 3 = local governments, n = number of respondents.

Note : The main countries represented in "Other" are: Japan (n=27), Singapore (n=11), Australia (n=11), United States (n=8), Malaysia (n=5).

Source: Asian Development Bank Client Perceptions Survey 2020.

Primary Clients

Figure 4 shows that nine in ten Primary Clients claim that they are familiar with ADB (90% are "very" or "somewhat" knowledgeable about ADB and its activities). This proportion is slightly higher than that recorded among all respondents.

Primary Clients from South Asia are the most likely to be "very" knowledgeable about ADB and its activities (40%).

The lowest level of familiarity, on the other hand, is recorded among private sector clients, one in four of which say that they are "not too knowledgeable" about ADB. There is room for ADB to increase ADB awareness and familiarity among clients in this area.

Figure 4: Familiarity with ADB, Primary Clients (%)

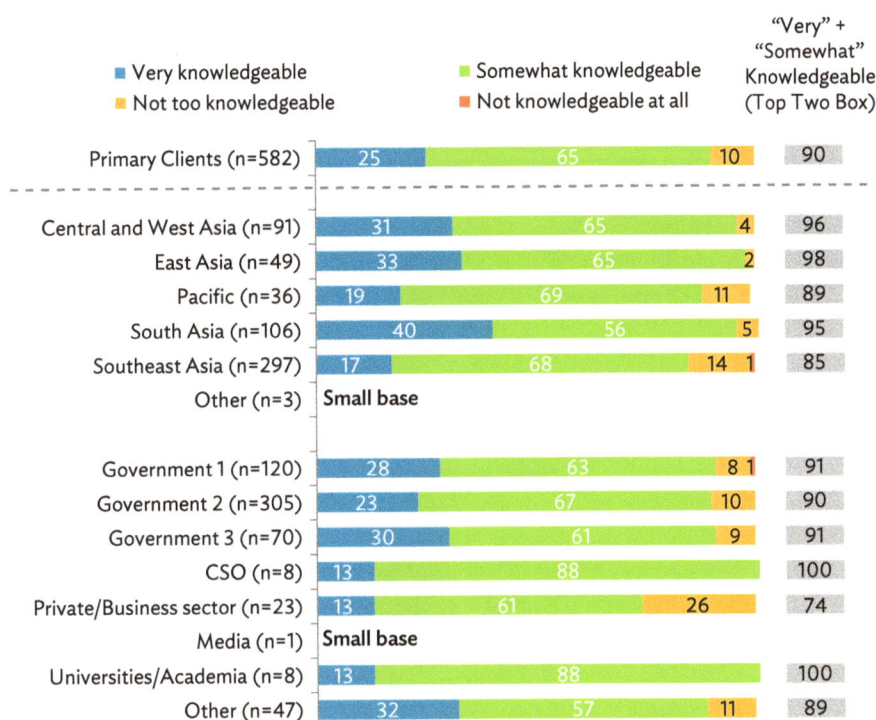

Legend:
- Very knowledgeable
- Somewhat knowledgeable
- Not too knowledgeable
- Not knowledgeable at all

Group	Very knowledgeable	Somewhat knowledgeable	Not too knowledgeable	Not knowledgeable at all	"Very" + "Somewhat" Knowledgeable (Top Two Box)
Primary Clients (n=582)	25	65	10		90
Central and West Asia (n=91)	31	65	4		96
East Asia (n=49)	33	65	2		98
Pacific (n=36)	19	69	11		89
South Asia (n=106)	40	56	5		95
Southeast Asia (n=297)	17	68	14	1	85
Other (n=3)	Small base				
Government 1 (n=120)	28	63	8	1	91
Government 2 (n=305)	23	67	10		90
Government 3 (n=70)	30	61	9		91
CSO (n=8)	13	88			100
Private/Business sector (n=23)	13	61	26		74
Media (n=1)	Small base				
Universities/Academia (n=8)	13	88			100
Other (n=47)	32	57	11		89

ADB = Asian Development Bank, CSO = civil society organization, Government 1 = central government, Government 2 = line ministries, Government 3 = local governments, n = number of respondents.

Note: Small base: n<5. "Other" pertains to respondents outside the listed group.

Source: Asian Development Bank Client Perceptions Survey 2020.

4 Overall Image of ADB

Clients mainly describe ADB as knowledgeable, trustworthy, and reliable, according to Figure 5.

Among all respondents, ADB is mostly regarded as knowledgeable (88% "strongly agree" or "agree"), trustworthy (87%), reliable (86%), and collaborative (85%).

Primary Clients perceive ADB similarly, with stronger associations among these four attributes (91% each) and ADB. A forward-looking attitude and transparency are also standout ADB attributes among Primary Clients (88% each), but less so among all respondents.

Among all respondents, while ADB is mainly viewed as knowledgeable, trustworthy, and reliable among most client groups, its image among clients in the media sector is slightly different. A collaborative approach is among the top three attributes associated with ADB by clients in government organizations.

For Primary Clients in government, such an approach is a top perceived image of ADB.

Figure 5: Image of ADB on a Five-Point Scale
(Top two Box Score, "Strongly Agree" + "Agree"; %)

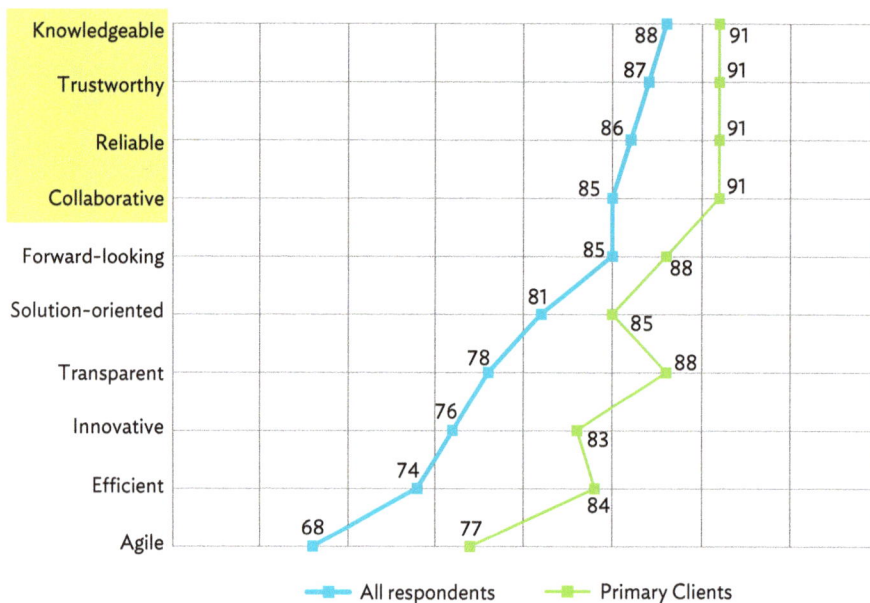

	All respondents	Primary Clients
Knowledgeable	88	91
Trustworthy	87	91
Reliable	86	91
Collaborative	85	91
Forward-looking	85	88
Solution-oriented	81	85
Transparent	78	88
Innovative	76	83
Efficient	74	84
Agile	68	77

ADB = Asian Development Bank.
Note: Survey base – entities familiar with ADB. Total no. of respondents = 1,214. Total no. of Primary Clients = 580.
Source: Asian Development Bank Client Perceptions Survey 2020.

5

Perceptions of ADB Knowledge Products, Services, and Events

Familiarity with ADB KPS

All Respondents

The majority of clients surveyed say they are generally familiar with ADB knowledge products, services, and events (75% are "very" or "moderately" knowledgeable about ADB KPS), as can be seen in Figure 6.

Clients in South Asia are more familiar with ADB knowledge content and activities than all the respondents combined (83% claim that they are "very" or "moderately" familiar). On the other hand, clients in the Pacific subregion and "other" regions are less familiar with ADB KPS (60% and 61%, respectively).

Among the client groups, those in the Government 3 group and in other organizations are the most familiar with ADB KPS (80%). It is worth noting that 27% of clients in the private sector are "not very" familiar with ADB KPS. This indicates potential for strengthening awareness of ADB knowledge products, services, and events among clients in this group.

Figure 6: Familiarity with ADB KPS, All Respondents (%)

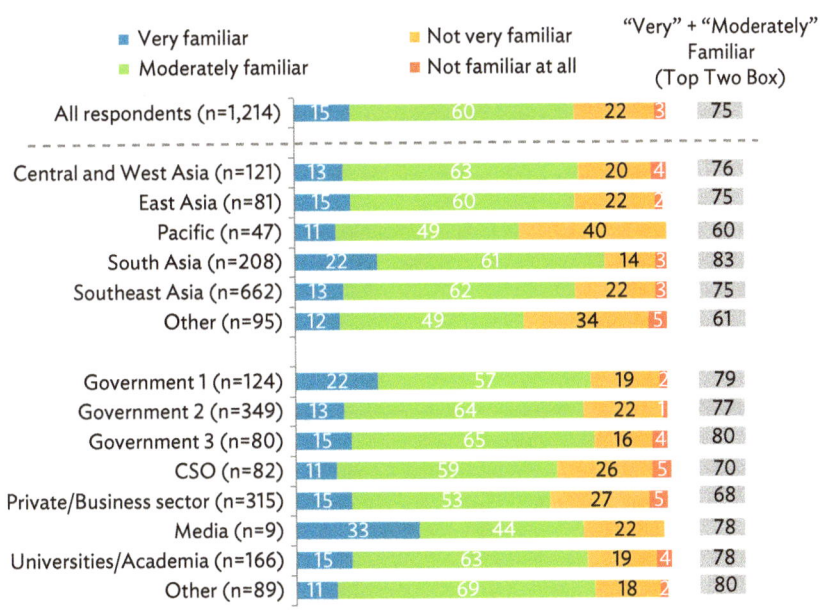

	Very familiar	Moderately familiar	Not very familiar	Not familiar at all	"Very" + "Moderately" Familiar (Top Two Box)
All respondents (n=1,214)	15	60	22	3	75
Central and West Asia (n=121)	13	63	20	4	76
East Asia (n=81)	15	60	22	2	75
Pacific (n=47)	11	49	40		60
South Asia (n=208)	22	61	14	3	83
Southeast Asia (n=662)	13	62	22	3	75
Other (n=95)	12	49	34	5	61
Government 1 (n=124)	22	57	19	2	79
Government 2 (n=349)	13	64	22	1	77
Government 3 (n=80)	15	65	16	4	80
CSO (n=82)	11	59	26	5	70
Private/Business sector (n=315)	15	53	27	5	68
Media (n=9)	33	44	22		78
Universities/Academia (n=166)	15	63	19	4	78
Other (n=89)	11	69	18	2	80

ADB = Asian Development Bank, CSO = civil society organization, Government 1 = central government, Government 2 = line ministries, Government 3 = local governments, KPS = knowledge products and services, n = number of respondents.

Note: Survey base – entities familiar with ADB.

Source: Asian Development Bank Client Perceptions Survey 2020.

Primary Clients

Figure 7 shows that nearly eight in ten Primary Clients claim familiarity with ADB knowledge products, services, and events (78% are "very" or "moderately" familiar). This proportion is slightly higher than that recorded among all respondents.

Primary Clients in South Asia are the most likely to be "very" familiar with ADB KPS (19%), and while those in the Pacific subregion have a lower level of familiarity (61% are "very" or "moderately" familiar) than the respondent group as a whole.

The level of familiarity is relatively high among all Primary Client groups, but it is lowest among clients in the private sector, with about one in four (26%) saying they are "not very" familiar with ADB KPS.

Performance

Usage

Figure 8 shows that among ADB KPS, webinars, seminars, workshops, and conferences are the most used by all ADB clients in general (75%) and by Primary Clients. Books, studies, reports, and working papers rank second (58%).

Primary Clients also mostly use webinars, seminars, workshops, and conferences (70%) among ADB KPS. However, they use significantly more capacity building / training than all respondents as a whole (63% vs. 45%), and also more process and project management / technical capacity development (46% vs. 34%).

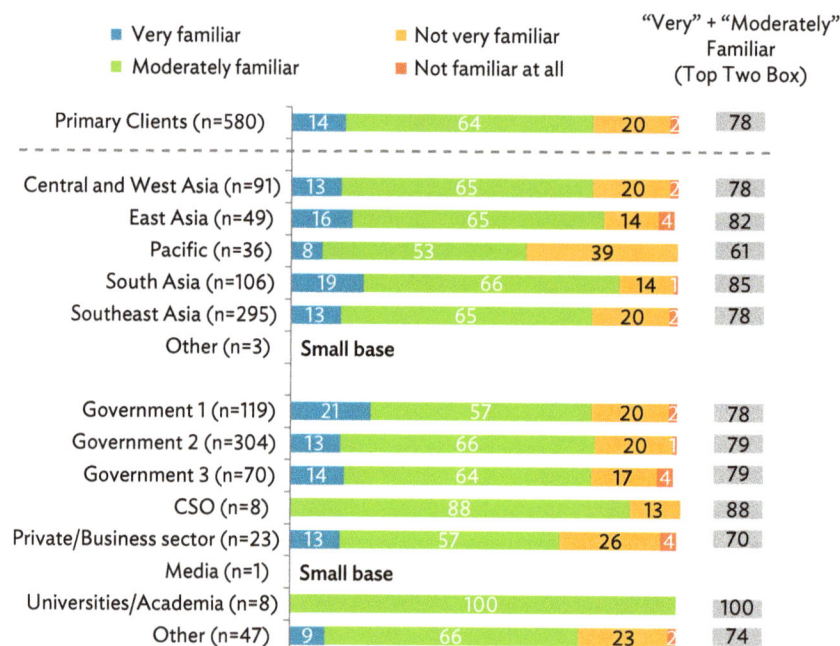

Figure 7: Familiarity with ADB KPS, Primary Clients
(%)

Legend:
- Very familiar
- Moderately familiar
- Not very familiar
- Not familiar at all

"Very" + "Moderately" Familiar (Top Two Box)

Group	Very familiar	Moderately familiar	Not very familiar	Not familiar at all	Top Two Box
Primary Clients (n=580)	14	64	20	2	78
Central and West Asia (n=91)	13	65	20	2	78
East Asia (n=49)	16	65	14	4	82
Pacific (n=36)	8	53	39		61
South Asia (n=106)	19	66	14	1	85
Southeast Asia (n=295)	13	65	20	2	78
Other (n=3)	Small base				
Government 1 (n=119)	21	57	20	2	78
Government 2 (n=304)	13	66	20	1	79
Government 3 (n=70)	14	64	17	4	79
CSO (n=8)		88	13		88
Private/Business sector (n=23)	13	57	26	4	70
Media (n=1)	Small base				
Universities/Academia (n=8)		100			100
Other (n=47)	9	66	23	2	74

ADB = Asian Development Bank, CSO = civil society organization, Government 1 = central government, Government 2 = line ministries, Government 3 = local governments, KPS = knowledge products and services, n = number of respondents.
Note: Survey base – entities familiar with ADB. Small base: n<5. "Other" pertains to respondents outside the listed group.
Source: Asian Development Bank Client Perceptions Survey 2020.

Figure 8: Use of ADB KPS at Work, All Respondents
(%)

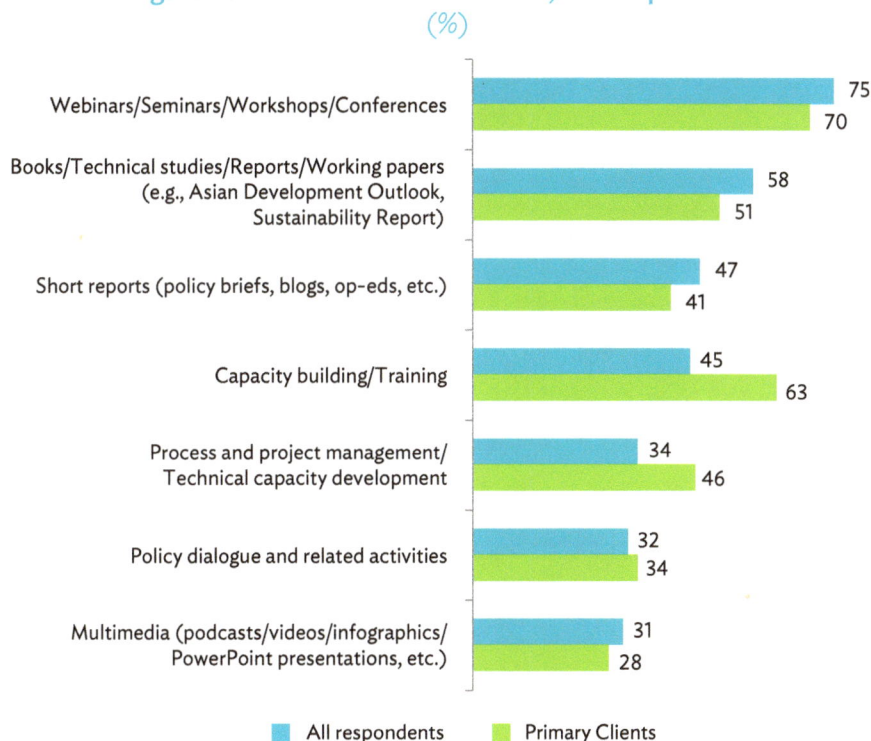

Category	All respondents	Primary Clients
Webinars/Seminars/Workshops/Conferences	75	70
Books/Technical studies/Reports/Working papers (e.g., Asian Development Outlook, Sustainability Report)	58	51
Short reports (policy briefs, blogs, op-eds, etc.)	47	41
Capacity building/Training	45	63
Process and project management/ Technical capacity development	34	46
Policy dialogue and related activities	32	34
Multimedia (podcasts/videos/infographics/ PowerPoint presentations, etc.)	31	28

■ All respondents   ■ Primary Clients

ADB = Asian Development Bank, KPS = knowledge products and services.

Note: Survey base – entities familiar with ADB knowledge products, services, and events. Total no. of respondents = 1,178. Total no. of Primary Clients = 570.

Source: Asian Development Bank Client Perceptions Survey 2020.

Usefulness

Almost all respondents and Primary Clients surveyed (99%) consider ADB KPS "extremely," "very," or "somewhat" useful. The most useful KPS, according to ADB clients, are capacity building/training and books, studies, reports, and working papers. Capacity building/Training stands out for being "extremely" useful to more than four in ten clients who use this service (41% of all respondents and 43% of Primary Clients), as can be seen in Figure 9.

ADB knowledge products, services, and events have similar usefulness ratings among Primary Clients and all respondents (78% of all respondents and 81% of the Primary Clients rate ADB KPS "extremely" or "very" useful; see Figure 10).

Among the various client groups, ADB KPS are most useful to the Government 1 group and least useful to clients in the private sector.

Figure 9: Usefulness of ADB KPS, All Respondents and Primary Clients
(%)

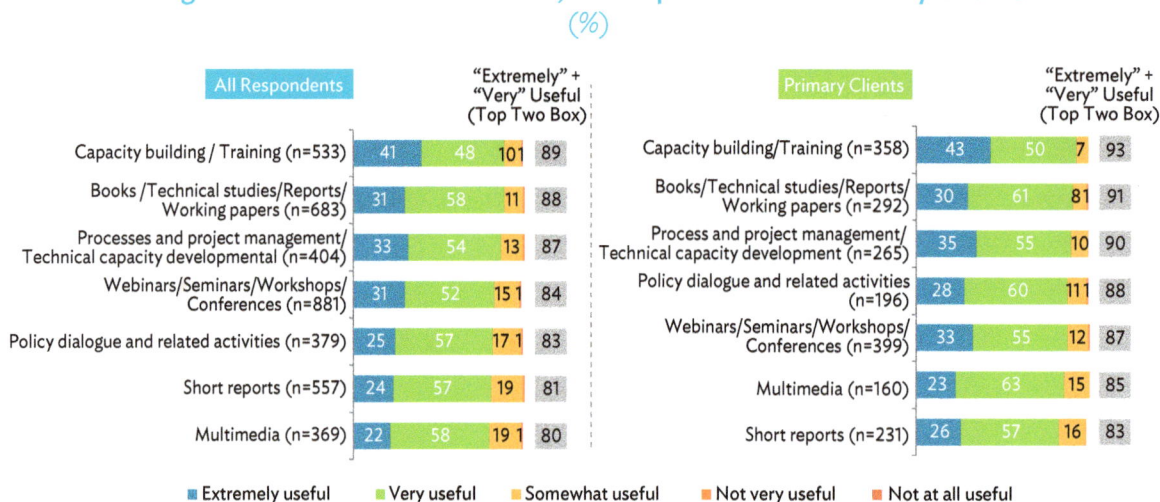

All Respondents — "Extremely" + "Very" Useful (Top Two Box)

Category	Extremely	Very	Somewhat	Not very	Not at all	Top Two Box
Capacity building / Training (n=533)	41	48	10	1		89
Books /Technical studies/Reports/ Working papers (n=683)	31	58	11			88
Processes and project management/ Technical capacity developmental (n=404)	33	54	13			87
Webinars/Seminars/Workshops/ Conferences (n=881)	31	52	15	1		84
Policy dialogue and related activities (n=379)	25	57	17	1		83
Short reports (n=557)	24	57	19			81
Multimedia (n=369)	22	58	19	1		80

Primary Clients — "Extremely" + "Very" Useful (Top Two Box)

Category	Extremely	Very	Somewhat	Not very	Not at all	Top Two Box
Capacity building/Training (n=358)	43	50	7			93
Books/Technical studies/Reports/ Working papers (n=292)	30	61	8	1		91
Process and project management/ Technical capacity development (n=265)	35	55	10			90
Policy dialogue and related activities (n=196)	28	60	11	1		88
Webinars/Seminars/Workshops/ Conferences (n=399)	33	55	12			87
Multimedia (n=160)	23	63	15			85
Short reports (n=231)	26	57	16			83

■ Extremely useful ■ Very useful ■ Somewhat useful ■ Not very useful ■ Not at all useful

ADB = Asian Development Bank, KPS = knowledge products and services, n = number of respondents.
Note: Survey base – users of the ADB knowledge product, service, or event.
Source: Asian Development Bank Client Perceptions Survey 2020.

Figure 10: Overall Usefulness of ADB KPS
(%)

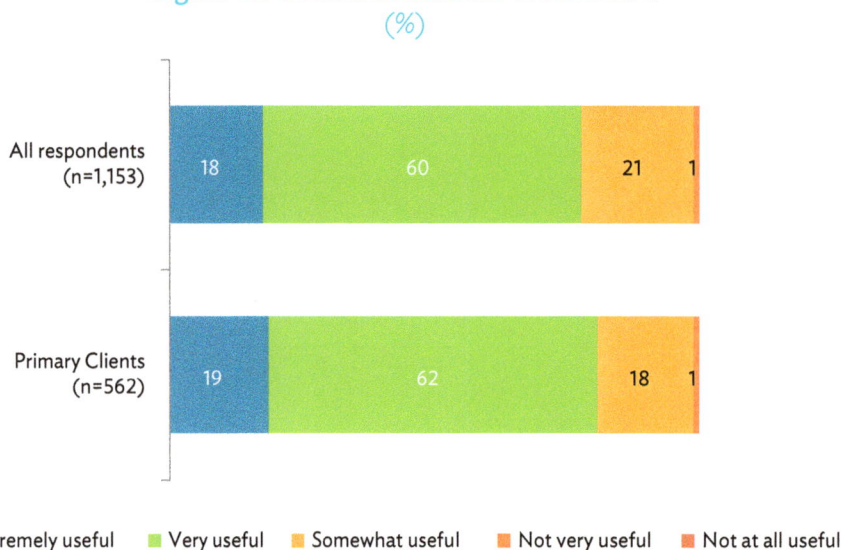

	Extremely	Very	Somewhat	Not very
All respondents (n=1,153)	18	60	21	1
Primary Clients (n=562)	19	62	18	1

■ Extremely useful ■ Very useful ■ Somewhat useful ■ Not very useful ■ Not at all useful

ADB = Asian Development Bank, KPS = knowledge products and services, n = number of respondents.
Note: Survey base – users of at least one ADB knowledge product, service, or event.
Source: Asian Development Bank Client Perceptions Survey 2020.

Clients' positive ratings for the overall usefulness of ADB KPS (Figure 11) are driven mainly by the "high quality of knowledge/data/information made available" and the "useful support for policy making and decision making" that ADB provides. Products that are "inapplicable/superficial" and "inaccessible" account for the most part for the negative ratings.

Usage versus Usefulness

ADB knowledge products, services, and events are all considered useful, but as Figure 12 shows, their levels of use vary.

Books, studies, reports, working papers, webinars, seminars, workshops, and conferences are all used efficiently by a majority of clients, and rank among the most useful KPS.

On the other hand, short reports, capacity building / training, and process/project management and technical capacity development, as well as multimedia and policy dialogue and related activities, although also deemed highly useful by ADB clients, have been used by less than half. Encouraging more clients to use these products and showcasing their usefulness in clients' work could expand product reach.

Among Primary Clients, ADB KPS are all considered useful; however, KPS usage by Primary Clients differs from usage among all respondents. Unlike the broader group of respondents, Primary Clients use capacity building / training to a great extent and consider it the most useful among all ADB KPS. But books, studies, reports, and working papers, despite being seen as very useful, are used by only half of the Primary Clients, and other ADB KPS, also considered highly useful,

Figure 11: Top 12 Reasons Given for Overall Usefulness Rating of ADB KPS (Open-Ended Question)
(%)

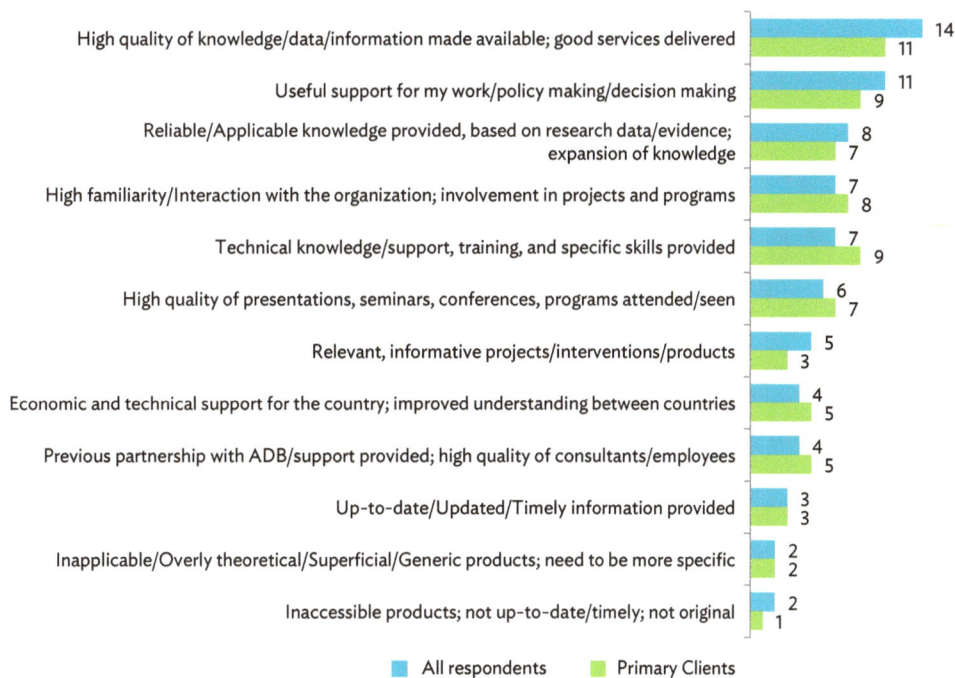

ADB = Asian Development Bank, KPS = knowledge products and services.
Note: Survey base – users of at least one ADB KPS in survey question Q2. Total no. of respondents = 1,153. Total no. of Primary Clients = 562.
Source: Asian Development Bank Client Perceptions Survey 2020.

Figure 12: ADB KPS Usage vs. Usefulness, All Respondents
(%)

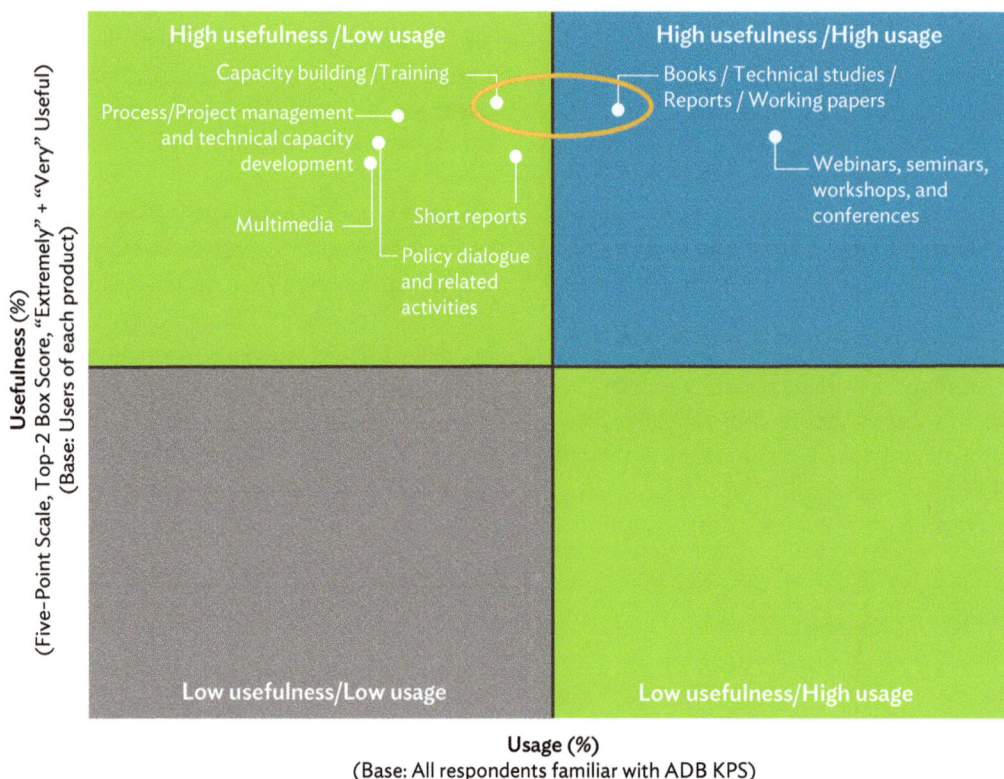

ADB = Asian Development Bank, KPS = knowledge products and services.

Note: Survey base – all respondents. "Usage" refers to the use of ADB knowledge products, services, and events, and to the consequent familiarity with the KPS. "Usefulness" refers to the utility of helpfulness of the KPS to their users.

Source: Asian Development Bank Client Perceptions Survey 2020.

are used by less than half. This leaves room to widen the use of these KPS.

ADB KPS are perceived to be useful both for tasks related to policies, programs, and projects (particularly design and implementation) and for the development of learning materials. Overall, Primary Clients are more likely to find ADB KPS useful in their work than all survey respondents.

Timeliness of Delivery

The majority of clients surveyed, particularly those in the Government 3 group and in universities and/or academia, agree that ADB KPS are delivered in a timely manner (66%).

Primary Clients are slightly more likely to rate the timeliness of delivery "excellent" or "good" (70%, vs. 66% of all survey respondents).

There is an appreciable gap in timeliness ratings among private sector respondents: 67% of Primary Clients rate the delivery of ADB KPS "excellent" or "good," compared with 55% of all respondents in the sector.

Application and Benefits

Figure 13 shows that the vast majority of ADB KPS users have applied information from the KPS in their work and say they have benefited from the use of these products and services.

Among all respondents, the main perceived benefit is the availability of data for use in policies/reports,

followed by the knowledge gained through capacity building and training. For Primary Clients, this increased knowledge and the improvements made possible in project design and implementation stand out as the top benefits of ADB KPS use.

Main Reasons behind Client Satisfaction with ADB KPS

Clients' satisfaction with ADB KPS covers many aspects including: timeliness and quality of knowledge obtained (main perceived benefit);

Figure 13: Application and Benefits of ADB KPS

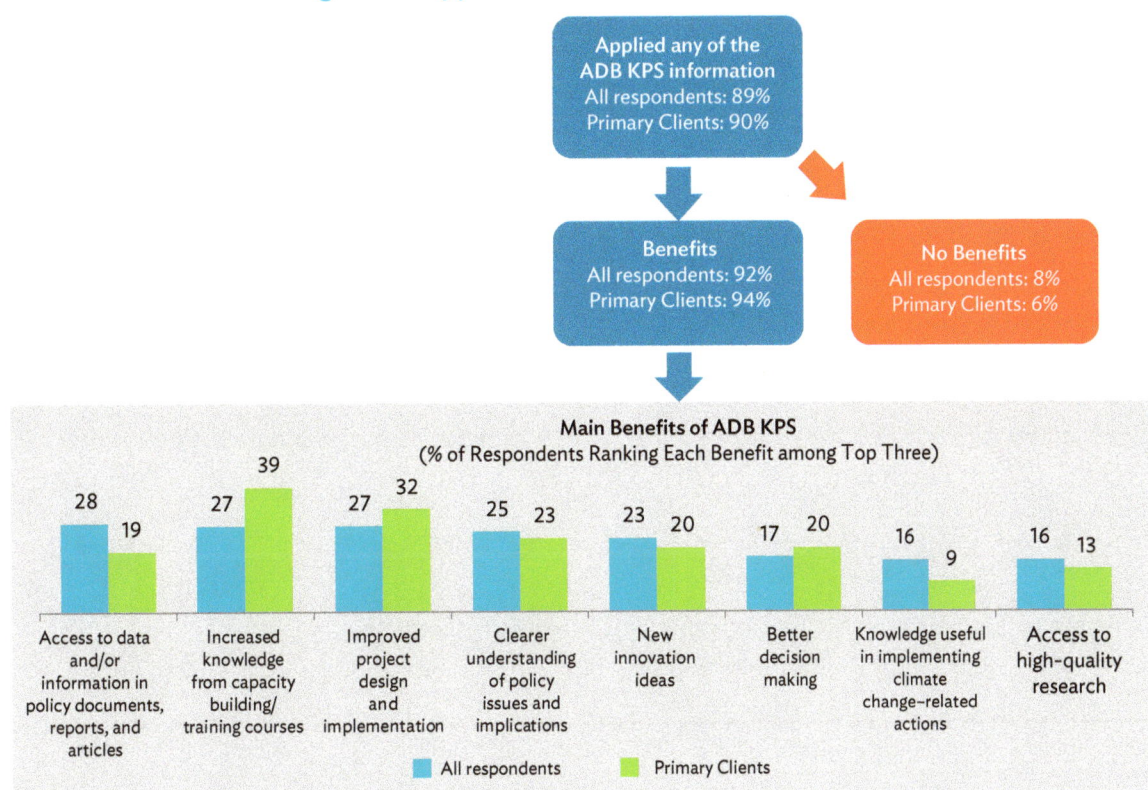

Applied any of the ADB KPS information
All respondents: 89%
Primary Clients: 90%

Benefits
All respondents: 92%
Primary Clients: 94%

No Benefits
All respondents: 8%
Primary Clients: 6%

Main Benefits of ADB KPS
(% of Respondents Ranking Each Benefit among Top Three)

Benefit	All respondents	Primary Clients
Access to data and/or information in policy documents, reports, and articles	28	19
Increased knowledge from capacity building/ training courses	27	39
Improved project design and implementation	27	32
Clearer understanding of policy issues and implications	25	23
New innovation ideas	23	20
Better decision making	17	20
Knowledge useful in implementing climate change–related actions	16	9
Access to high-quality research	16	13

ADB = Asian Development Bank, KPS = knowledge products and services.
Note: Survey base – users of at least one ADB KPS in survey question Q2. All respondents = 1,129 for survey question Q8, 1,002 for survey question Q9a, and 904 for survey question Q9b. Primary Clients = 549 for survey question Q8, 495 for survey question Q9a, and 459 for survey question Q9b.
Source: Asian Development Bank Client Perceptions Survey 2020.

ADB's development effectiveness, responsiveness, and collaboration with development partners (three CRF tracking indicators); and knowledge support for the fight against the coronavirus disease (COVID-19). This survey report further analyzes how all these dimensions correlate with clients' overall satisfaction with ADB KPS.

The impact of ADB KPS on program/project design and implementation is the most important factor in overall satisfaction, followed by self-education and policy/program advice. Success in these three areas is driven mainly by capacity building/training, and is based on sound data and analytics, as well as on other information found in books/technical studies/reports/working papers. Without capacity building /training support, the impact of the data and other information is greatly reduced.

The most important factor in overall satisfaction is timeliness. It drives overall satisfaction directly and underlies the usefulness of all other KPS elements. For example, training and technical papers are useful when offered at the right time.

In conclusion, timely capacity building/training based on a solid foundation of relevant and most recent data and analytics (e.g., from books, technical studies, working papers, reports) useful in policy/program design and implementation, and in professional self-development, can most improve clients' satisfaction with ADB KPS.

Continuous efforts should be put into making ADB KPS less theoretical and generic, and more timely and accessible, and increasing the use of some KPS, such as process/project management, technical capacity development, short reports, multimedia, and policy dialogue.

6

Perceptions of ADBI Knowledge Products, Services, and Events

Familiarity

As can be seen in Figure 14, seven in ten respondents claim some familiarity with ADBI and its activities (70% are "very" or "somewhat" knowledgeable).

Clients in the Government 1 group and in the media sector are the most familiar with ADBI and its activities (77% and 93%, respectively). Private sector clients, on the other hand, are less familiar (63%) than all respondents.

Among respondents familiar with ADBI ("very" or "somewhat" knowledgeable about ADBI), two-thirds (67%) are "very" or "moderately" familiar with ADBI policy dialogues, training programs, e-learning courses, and other capacity-building products, as shown in Figure 15.

Figure 14: Familiarity with ADBI, All Respondents
(%)

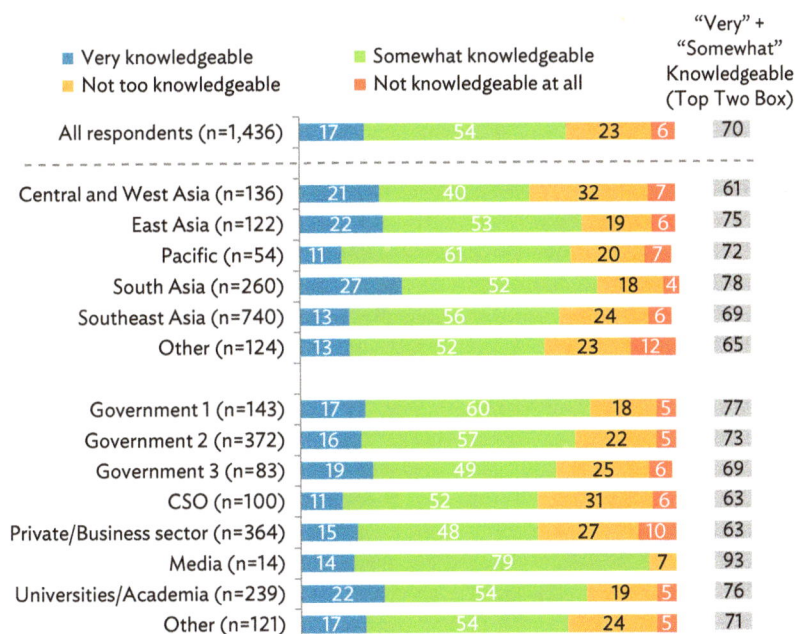

ADB = Asian Development Bank, ADBI = Asian Development Bank Institute, CSO = civil society organization, Government 1 = central government, Government 2 = line ministries, Government 3 = local governments, n = number of respondents.

Note: All respondents are composed of 1,216 from the ADB database and 220 from ADBI database. "Other" pertains to respondents outside the listed group.

Source: Asian Development Bank Client Perceptions Survey 2020.

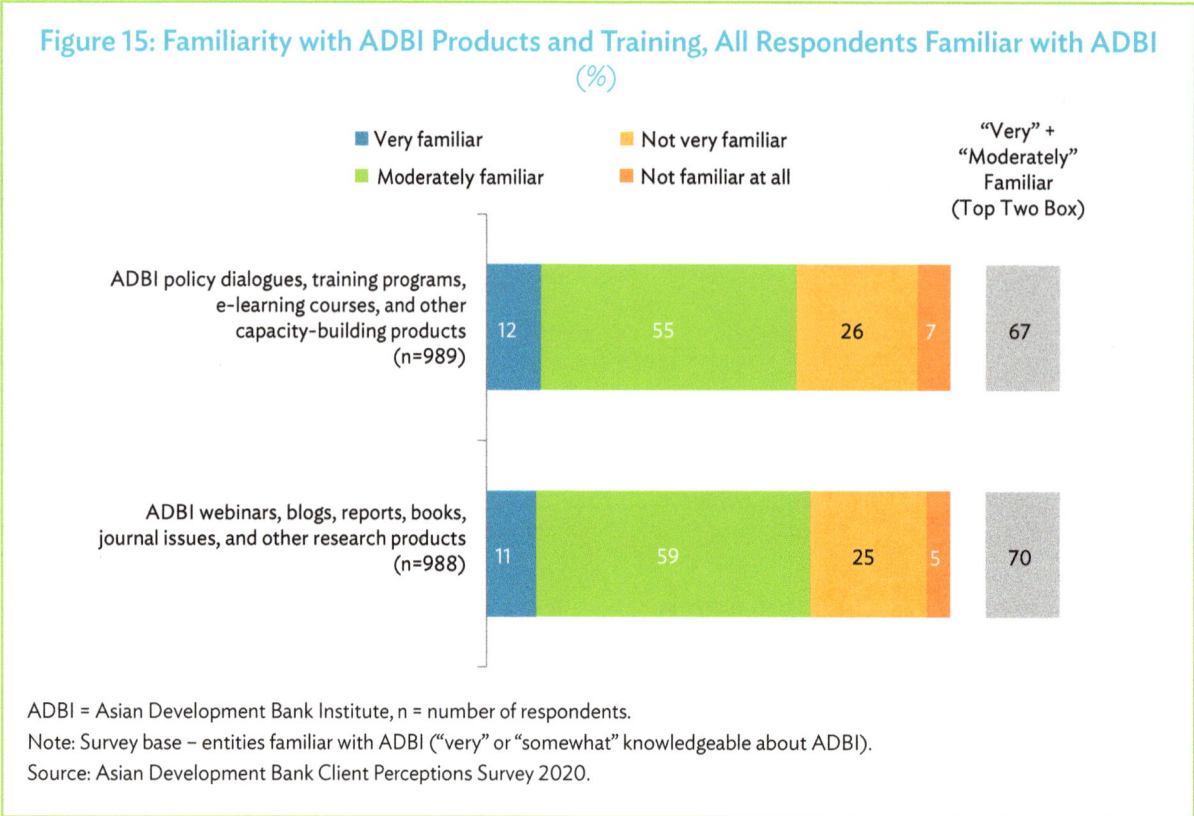

Figure 15: Familiarity with ADBI Products and Training, All Respondents Familiar with ADBI (%)

Legend:
- Very familiar
- Moderately familiar
- Not very familiar
- Not familiar at all
- "Very" + "Moderately" Familiar (Top Two Box)

ADBI policy dialogues, training programs, e-learning courses, and other capacity-building products (n=989): 12 | 55 | 26 | 7 — Top Two Box: 67

ADBI webinars, blogs, reports, books, journal issues, and other research products (n=988): 11 | 59 | 25 | 5 — Top Two Box: 70

ADBI = Asian Development Bank Institute, n = number of respondents.
Note: Survey base – entities familiar with ADBI ("very" or "somewhat" knowledgeable about ADBI).
Source: Asian Development Bank Client Perceptions Survey 2020.

ADBI products and training are well known among respondents familiar with ADBI: two-thirds (67%) are "very" or "moderately" familiar with ADBI policy dialogues, training programs, e-learning courses, and other capacity-building products.

Respondents familiar with ADBI have a similar level of familiarity with ADBI webinars, blogs, reports, books, journal issues, and other research products.

Relevance to Work

Figure 16 shows that ADBI research webinars, seminars, workshops, and conferences are considered "extremely" or "very" relevant by 69% of respondents familiar with ADBI. The other types of ADBI KPS that are rated most relevant are books, reports, and journal issues (66% of respondents find these relevant to their work) and short publications (64%).

With 21% saying they are not familiar with ADBI e-learning courses, awareness of these products can be increased to improve their relevance.

Importance of Work Tasks

Tasks related to designing and implementing policies, programs, or projects are considered the most important in respondents' work. Respondents rate these tasks "extremely" or "very" important in their work (76% each, for both design and implementation). Preparing policy or program advice is rated nearly as high (72%), as shown in Figure 17.

Figure 16: Relevance of ADBI Knowledge Products, Services, and Events, All Respondents Familiar with ADBI
(%)

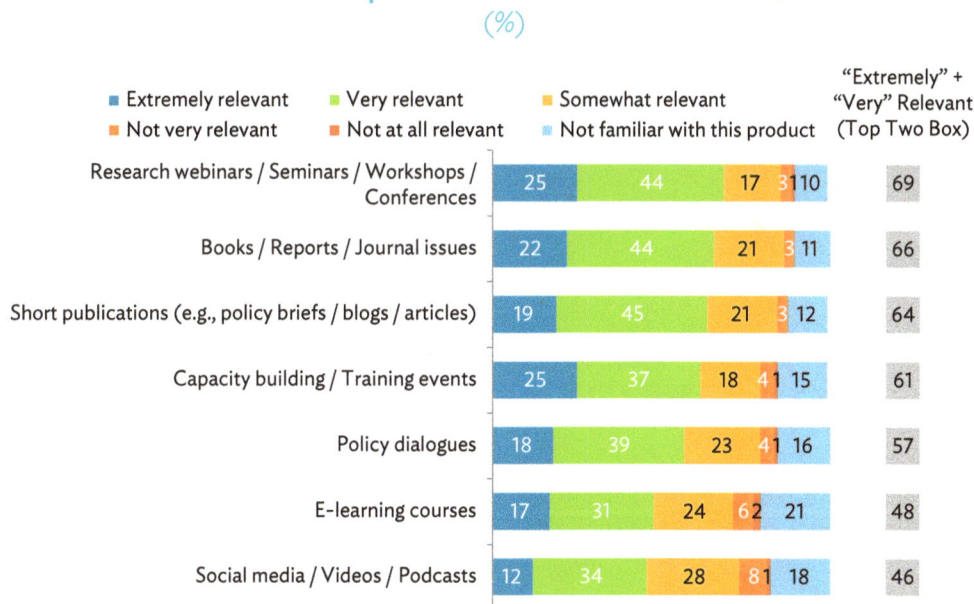

- ■ Extremely relevant
- ■ Very relevant
- ■ Somewhat relevant
- ■ Not very relevant
- ■ Not at all relevant
- ■ Not familiar with this product

"Extremely" + "Very" Relevant (Top Two Box)

Product	Extremely relevant	Very relevant	Somewhat relevant	Not very relevant	Not at all relevant	Not familiar with this product	Top Two Box
Research webinars / Seminars / Workshops / Conferences	25	44	17	3	1	10	69
Books / Reports / Journal issues	22	44	21	3		11	66
Short publications (e.g., policy briefs / blogs / articles)	19	45	21	3		12	64
Capacity building / Training events	25	37	18	4	1	15	61
Policy dialogues	18	39	23	4	1	16	57
E-learning courses	17	31	24	6	2	21	48
Social media / Videos / Podcasts	12	34	28	8		18	46

ADBI = Asian Development Bank Institute.
Note: Survey base – entities familiar with ADBI. All respondents = 982 (762 from ADB database and 220 from ADBI database).
Source: Asian Development Bank Client Perceptions Survey 2020.

Figure 17: Importance of Work Tasks, All Respondents
(%)

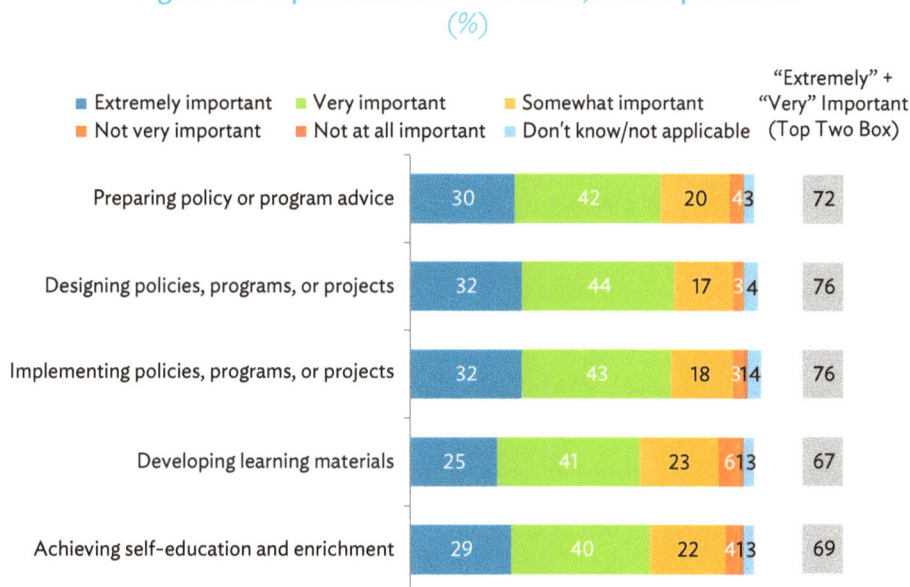

- ■ Extremely important
- ■ Very important
- ■ Somewhat important
- ■ Not very important
- ■ Not at all important
- ■ Don't know/not applicable

"Extremely" + "Very" Important (Top Two Box)

Task	Extremely important	Very important	Somewhat important	Not very important	Not at all important	Don't know/not applicable	Top Two Box
Preparing policy or program advice	30	42	20	4		3	72
Designing policies, programs, or projects	32	44	17	3		4	76
Implementing policies, programs, or projects	32	43	18	3	1	4	76
Developing learning materials	25	41	23	6	1	3	67
Achieving self-education and enrichment	29	40	22	4	1	3	69

ADB = Asian Development Bank, ADBI = Asian Development Bank Institute.
Note: Survey base – entities familiar with at least one ADBI product, service, or event. All respondents = 902 (684 from ADB database and 218 from ADB database).
Source: Asian Development Bank Client Perceptions Survey 2020.

Gaining knowledge is also considered important by two-thirds of respondents familiar with ADBI: 69% agree that achieving self-education and enrichment is "extremely" or "very" important in their work, while 67% say the same thing about developing learning materials.

Relevance of KPS to Work Tasks

According to Figure 18, respondents view ADBI's knowledge products, services, and events as relevant to some extent to their main work tasks.

Two-thirds of respondents agree that these KPS are relevant to designing and implementing policies, programs, and projects (65% and 64%, respectively, rate ADBI products "extremely" or "very" relevant to these tasks).

A majority also believe that the KPS are relevant to the development of new materials and to self-education (63% and 59%, respectively).

Relevance to Work Tasks in Relation to Importance of Work Tasks

Figure 19 shows that ADBI KPS are relevant to the main work activities and tasks of respondents.

The KPS are rated most relevant to tasks that are most important in the respondents' work—designing and implementing new policies, programs, or projects.

Self-education is considered relatively important. ADBI KPS could be more helpful in clients' learning and knowledge development.

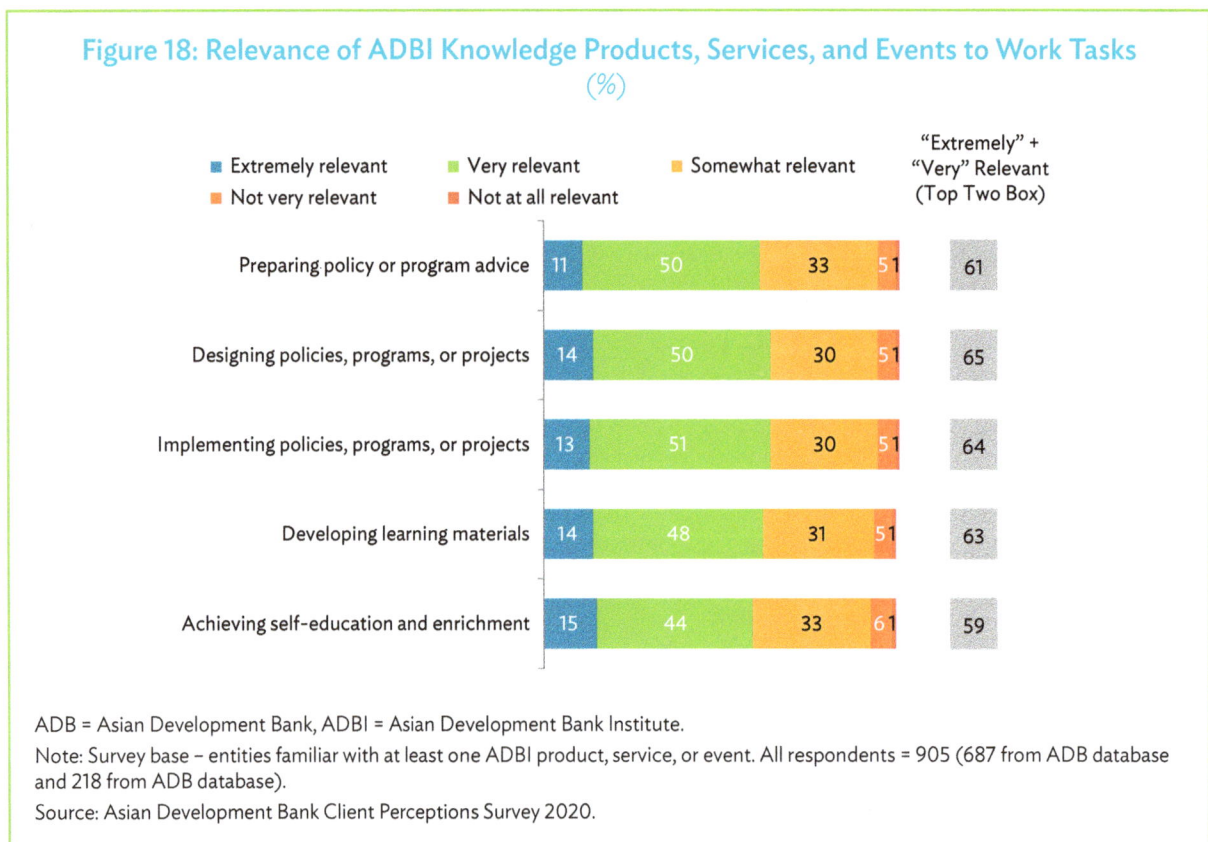

Figure 18: Relevance of ADBI Knowledge Products, Services, and Events to Work Tasks
(%)

Legend: Extremely relevant, Very relevant, Somewhat relevant, Not very relevant, Not at all relevant

Task	Extremely relevant	Very relevant	Somewhat relevant	Not very relevant	Not at all relevant	"Extremely" + "Very" Relevant (Top Two Box)
Preparing policy or program advice	11	50	33	5	1	61
Designing policies, programs, or projects	14	50	30	5	1	65
Implementing policies, programs, or projects	13	51	30	5	1	64
Developing learning materials	14	48	31	5	1	63
Achieving self-education and enrichment	15	44	33	6	1	59

ADB = Asian Development Bank, ADBI = Asian Development Bank Institute.
Note: Survey base – entities familiar with at least one ADBI product, service, or event. All respondents = 905 (687 from ADB database and 218 from ADB database).
Source: Asian Development Bank Client Perceptions Survey 2020.

Figure 19: Relevance of ADBI Knowledge Products, Services, and Events
to Work Activities vs. Importance of Work Tasks, All Respondents
(%)

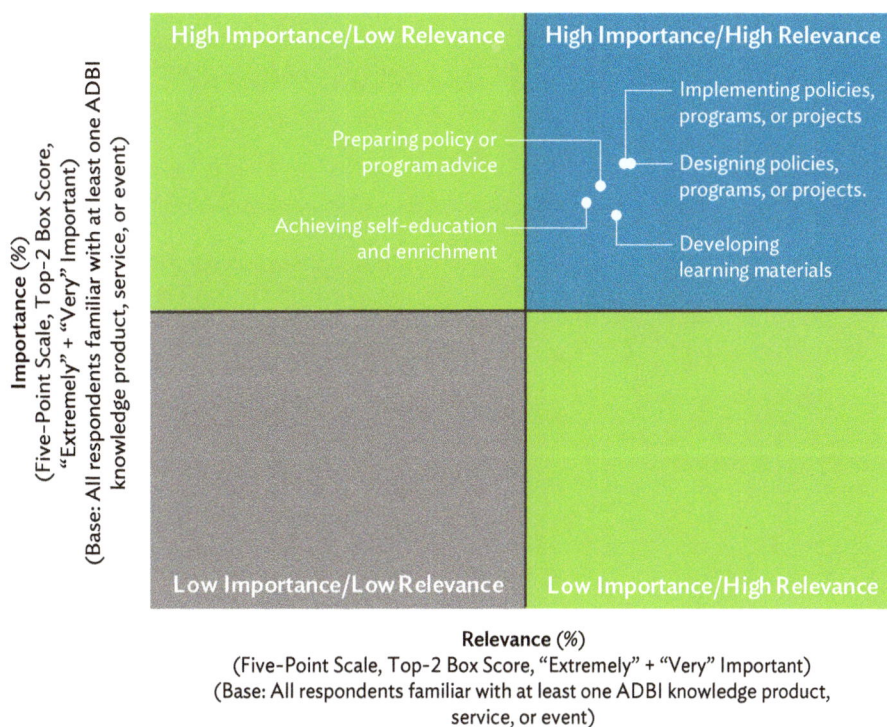

High Importance/Low Relevance	**High Importance/High Relevance**
Preparing policy or program advice	Implementing policies, programs, or projects
Achieving self-education and enrichment	Designing policies, programs, or projects.
	Developing learning materials
Low Importance/Low Relevance	**Low Importance/High Relevance**

Importance (%)
(Five-Point Scale, Top-2 Box Score, "Extremely" + "Very" Important)
(Base: All respondents familiar with at least one ADBI knowledge product, service, or event)

Relevance (%)
(Five-Point Scale, Top-2 Box Score, "Extremely" + "Very" Important)
(Base: All respondents familiar with at least one ADBI knowledge product, service, or event)

ADBI = Asian Development Bank Institute.
Note: Survey base – entities familiar with at least one ADBI product, service, or event. All respondents = 905 (question about relevance), 902 (question about importance).
Source: Asian Development Bank Client Perceptions Survey 2020.

Overall Relevance

As a whole, ADBI KPS are almost universally viewed as relevant: 96% of respondents say that these products are "extremely," "very," or "somewhat" relevant.

Two-thirds of respondents (64%) agree that ADBI KPS are "extremely" or "very" relevant. However, these products and services could be made more relevant to the needs of private sector clients.

The relative importance given to self-education suggests that ADBI KPS could further advance clients' learning and knowledge acquisition.

Perceived Benefits of ADBI KPS and Events

As Figure 20 shows, the vast majority of respondents familiar with ADBI regard the use of ADBI KPS as beneficial to their work.

Among all respondents, the main perceived benefits derived from using ADBI knowledge products and services relate mostly to policies and general learning. The possibility of using the data in policies, reports, or articles is the top perceived benefit (33%), followed by a clearer understanding of policy issues (32%).

The knowledge gained from capacity building and training is also considered a main benefit: it ranks among the top three recognized benefits (32%).

A majority of respondents familiar with ADBI agree that ADBI is an excellent source of knowledge of development issues (83%).

Figure 20: Benefits Gained from Using ADBI KPS

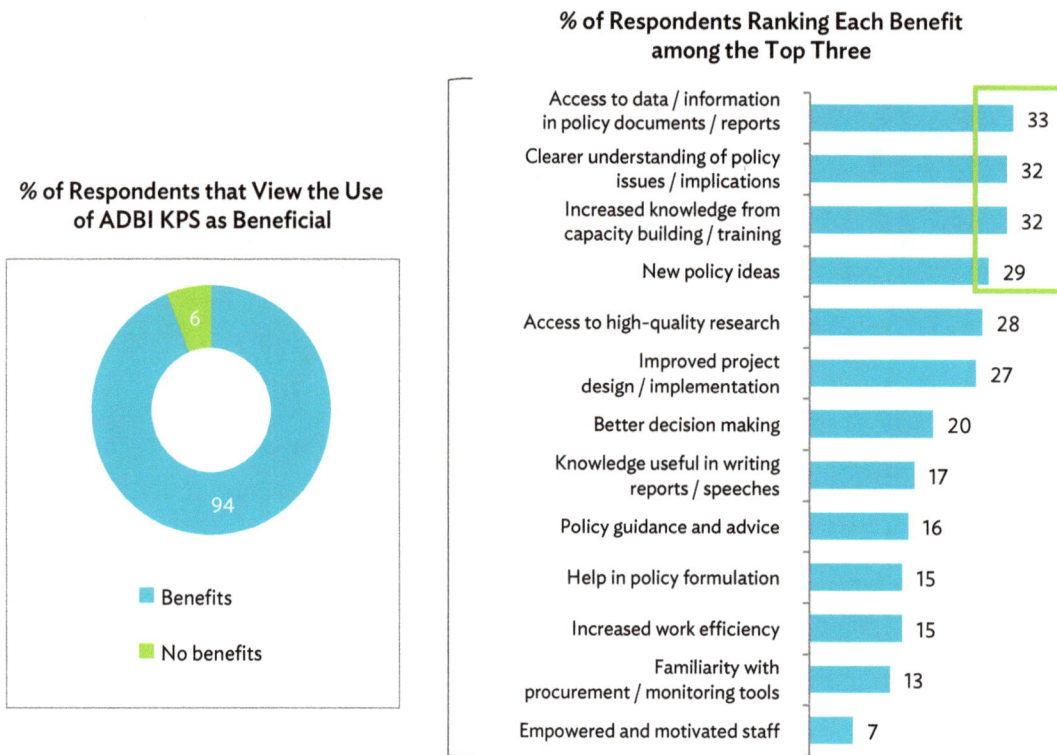

% of Respondents that View the Use of ADBI KPS as Beneficial

% of Respondents Ranking Each Benefit among the Top Three

Benefit	%
Access to data / information in policy documents / reports	33
Clearer understanding of policy issues / implications	32
Increased knowledge from capacity building / training	32
New policy ideas	29
Access to high-quality research	28
Improved project design / implementation	27
Better decision making	20
Knowledge useful in writing reports / speeches	17
Policy guidance and advice	16
Help in policy formulation	15
Increased work efficiency	15
Familiarity with procurement / monitoring tools	13
Empowered and motivated staff	7

Donut chart: Benefits 94, No benefits 6

■ Benefits
■ No benefits

ADBI = Asian Development Bank Institute, KPS = knowledge products and services.
Note: Survey base – entities familiar with at least one ADBI product, service, or event. All respondents = 901 (survey question Q6), 834 (survey question Q7).
Source: Asian Development Bank Client Perceptions Survey 2020.

7

Perceptions of ADB's Development and Organizational Effectiveness

Overview of Performance

A higher level of satisfaction with ADB's performance is recorded overall among Primary Clients versus all respondents.

Satisfaction with ADB's development effectiveness is relatively high (61% are "extremely" or "very" satisfied), particularly among Primary Clients (75%).

But, also as shown in Figure 21, only about half of all respondents say they are "extremely" or "very" satisfied with ADB's responsiveness when it comes to meeting their needs (52%) and with ADB's collaboration with development partners (54%), leaving room for increasing these levels of satisfaction.

Between 94% and 98% of Primary Clients and all respondents are "extremely," "very," or "somewhat" satisfied with ADB's performance (Figure 21).

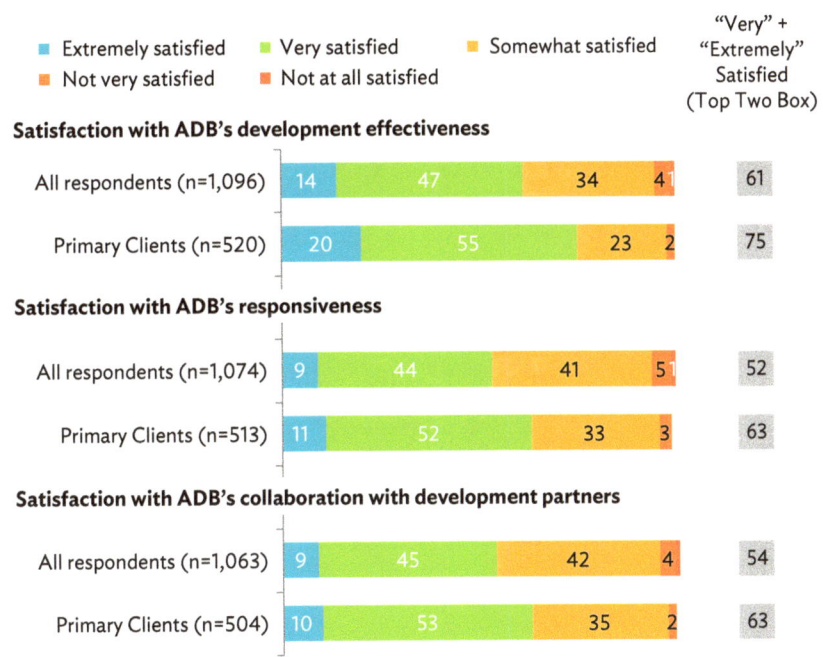

Figure 21: Satisfaction with ADB's Performance
(%)

Legend:
- Extremely satisfied
- Very satisfied
- Somewhat satisfied
- Not very satisfied
- Not at all satisfied

"Very" + "Extremely" Satisfied (Top Two Box)

Satisfaction with ADB's development effectiveness

	Extremely	Very	Somewhat	Not very	Top Two Box
All respondents (n=1,096)	14	47	34	4 1	61
Primary Clients (n=520)	20	55	23	2	75

Satisfaction with ADB's responsiveness

All respondents (n=1,074)	9	44	41	5 1	52
Primary Clients (n=513)	11	52	33	3	63

Satisfaction with ADB's collaboration with development partners

All respondents (n=1,063)	9	45	42	4	54
Primary Clients (n=504)	10	53	35	2	63

ADB = Asian Development Bank, n = number of respondents.
Note: Survey base – entities familiar with ADB.
Source: Asian Development Bank Client Perceptions Survey 2020.

Development Effectiveness

Clients surveyed (including those from "other" regions), particularly those in government organizations, are relatively satisfied with ADB's development effectiveness in their countries.

Among the subregions in Asia and the Pacific, there are some differences in the level of satisfaction with ADB's development effectiveness. A vast majority of clients in the Pacific subregion (83%) are "extremely" or "very" satisfied with the development results achieved by ADB in their country, while just over half (58%) in Southeast Asia share that view.

Likewise, as can be seen in Figure 22, there are major disparities among the different client groups. Clients in government organizations are highly satisfied, while less than half of those from CSOs or the private sector say that they are "extremely" or "very" satisfied with ADB's development effectiveness.

Figure 22: ADB's Development Effectiveness, All Respondents
(%)

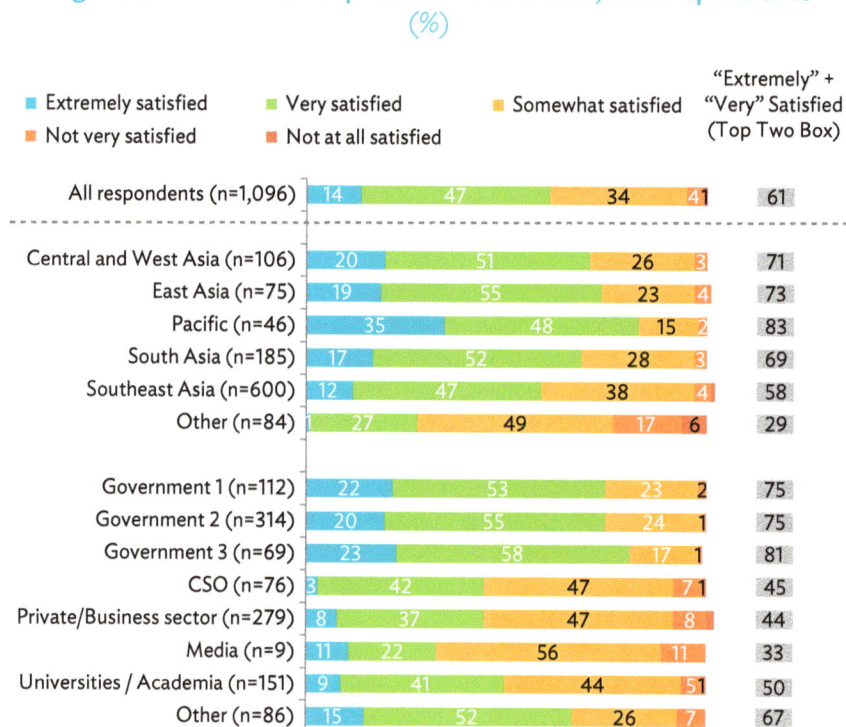

Legend:
- Extremely satisfied
- Very satisfied
- Somewhat satisfied
- Not very satisfied
- Not at all satisfied
- "Extremely" + "Very" Satisfied (Top Two Box)

Respondent	Extremely satisfied	Very satisfied	Somewhat satisfied	Not very satisfied	Not at all satisfied	"Extremely" + "Very" Satisfied (Top Two Box)
All respondents (n=1,096)	14	47	34	4	1	61
Central and West Asia (n=106)	20	51	26	3		71
East Asia (n=75)	19	55	23	4		73
Pacific (n=46)	35	48	15	2		83
South Asia (n=185)	17	52	28	3		69
Southeast Asia (n=600)	12	47	38	4		58
Other (n=84)	1	27	49	17	6	29
Government 1 (n=112)	22	53	23	2		75
Government 2 (n=314)	20	55	24	1		75
Government 3 (n=69)	23	58	17	1		81
CSO (n=76)	3	42	47	7	1	45
Private/Business sector (n=279)	8	37	47	8		44
Media (n=9)	11	22	56	11		33
Universities / Academia (n=151)	9	41	44	5	1	50
Other (n=86)	15	52	26	7		67

ADB = Asian Development Bank , CSO = civil society organization, Government 1 = central government, Government 2 = line ministries, Government 3 = local governments n = number of respondents.
Note: Survey base – entities familiar with ADB. "Other" pertains to respondents outside the listed group.
Source: Asian Development Bank Client Perceptions Survey 2020.

A majority of Primary Clients are satisfied with the help given by ADB to their country in achieving development results, with three in four (75%) stating that they are "extremely" or "very" satisfied (Figure 23).

Some differences are observed at the subregional and sector level:

- Primary Clients in the Pacific subregion drive client satisfaction, with 89% "extremely" or "very" satisfied. "Extremely" satisfied Primary Clients total 43%—the highest among all subregions.

- At the sector level, the satisfaction of Primary Clients in the private sector (only 50% are "extremely" or "very" satisfied) could be increased further.

Performance by Area

Figure 24 presents the areas for which ADB gets the highest performance ratings from clients, including Primary Clients: improving infrastructure, promoting environmental sustainability, and strengthening governance and institutional capacity.

The largest perception gap between all clients surveyed and Primary Clients exists in ADB's performance in strengthening governance and institutional capacity, which is rated "excellent" or "good" by 65% of all clients surveyed, compared with 77% of Primary Clients.

ADB's performance in improving education and training and providing integrated solutions to development challenges is also deemed noteworthy by Primary Clients (72% for the first performance area, and 71% for the second), but less so by all respondents (63% and 64%, respectively).

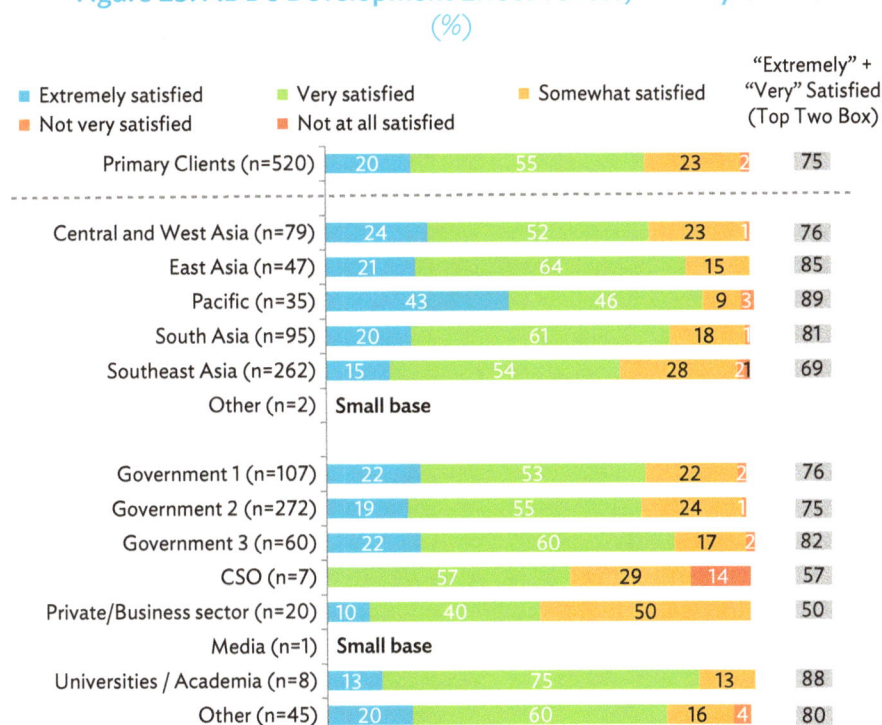

Figure 23: ADB's Development Effectiveness, Primary Clients
(%)

Legend:
- Extremely satisfied
- Very satisfied
- Somewhat satisfied
- Not very satisfied
- Not at all satisfied

"Extremely" + "Very" Satisfied (Top Two Box)

	Extremely	Very	Somewhat	Not very	Not at all	Top Two Box
Primary Clients (n=520)	20	55	23	2		75
Central and West Asia (n=79)	24	52	23	1		76
East Asia (n=47)	21	64	15			85
Pacific (n=35)	43	46	9	3		89
South Asia (n=95)	20	61	18	1		81
Southeast Asia (n=262)	15	54	28	2	1	69
Other (n=2)	Small base					
Government 1 (n=107)	22	53	22	2		76
Government 2 (n=272)	19	55	24	1		75
Government 3 (n=60)	22	60	17	2		82
CSO (n=7)		57	29		14	57
Private/Business sector (n=20)	10	40	50			50
Media (n=1)	Small base					
Universities / Academia (n=8)	13	75	13			88
Other (n=45)	20	60	16	4		80

ADB = Asian Development Bank , CSO = civil society organization, Government 1 = central government, Government 2 = line ministries, Government 3 = local governments, n = number of respondents.
Note: Survey base – entities familiar with ADB. Small base: n<5; "Other" pertains to respondents outside the listed group.
Source: Asian Development Bank Client Perceptions Survey 2020.

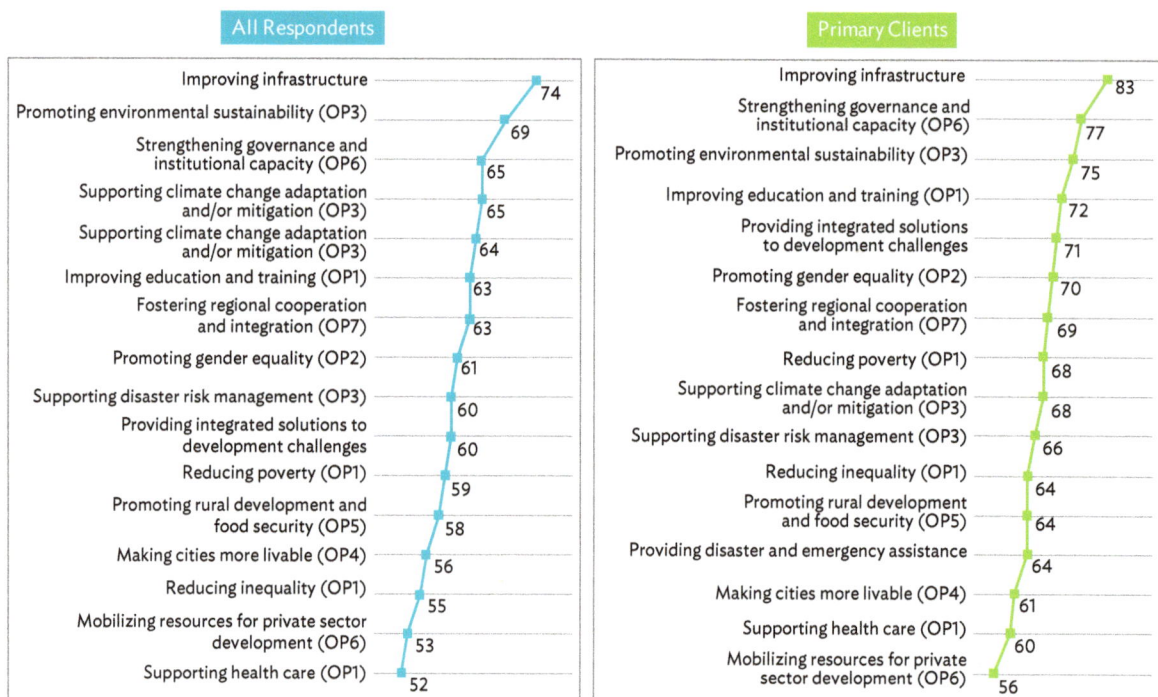

Figure 24: Performance of ADB on a Five-Point Scale
(Top two Box Score, "Excellent" + "Good"; %)

All Respondents

Improving infrastructure	74
Promoting environmental sustainability (OP3)	69
Strengthening governance and institutional capacity (OP6)	65
Supporting climate change adaptation and/or mitigation (OP3)	65
Supporting climate change adaptation and/or mitigation (OP3)	64
Improving education and training (OP1)	63
Fostering regional cooperation and integration (OP7)	63
Promoting gender equality (OP2)	61
Supporting disaster risk management (OP3)	60
Providing integrated solutions to development challenges	60
Reducing poverty (OP1)	59
Promoting rural development and food security (OP5)	58
Making cities more livable (OP4)	56
Reducing inequality (OP1)	55
Mobilizing resources for private sector development (OP6)	53
Supporting health care (OP1)	52

Primary Clients

Improving infrastructure	83
Strengthening governance and institutional capacity (OP6)	77
Promoting environmental sustainability (OP3)	75
Improving education and training (OP1)	72
Providing integrated solutions to development challenges	71
Promoting gender equality (OP2)	70
Fostering regional cooperation and integration (OP7)	69
Reducing poverty (OP1)	68
Supporting climate change adaptation and/or mitigation (OP3)	68
Supporting disaster risk management (OP3)	66
Reducing inequality (OP1)	64
Promoting rural development and food security (OP5)	64
Providing disaster and emergency assistance	64
Making cities more livable (OP4)	61
Supporting health care (OP1)	60
Mobilizing resources for private sector development (OP6)	56

ADB = Asian Development Bank, OP = Operational Priority.
Source: Asian Development Bank Client Perceptions Survey 2020.

Responsiveness

Figure 25 shows that half (52%) of clients surveyed (including those from "other" regions) are "extremely" or "very" satisfied with ADB's responsiveness to their needs.

There are large differences between client groups. Clients in government organizations are more likely to be satisfied with ADB's responsiveness (62%–72%) than those in the private sector, CSOs, and universities/academia (36%–43%).

Primary Clients, as shown in Figure 26, regard ADB as responsive to their needs: 63% say they are "extremely" or "very" satisfied with ADB's responsiveness.

Among the different client groups, the proportion of Primary Clients that are "extremely" or "very" satisfied with ADB's responsiveness varies widely: satisfaction is highest among Primary Clients in the Government 3 group (73%) and lowest among those in the private/business sector (25%).

Moreover, dissatisfaction is noted among 10% of Primary Clients in the private sector and among 14% of CSOs. This can and should be addressed.

The main drivers of ADB's positive responsiveness ratings are the suitability and timeliness of its response and its readiness to provide countries with "effective economic/infrastructure support," together with a good understanding of local problems (also the main reasons given by Primary Clients). Low familiarity with ADB and inadequacy of the ADB response account for the most part for the negative ratings, as shown in Figure 27.

Figure 25: ADB Responsiveness, All Respondents
(%)

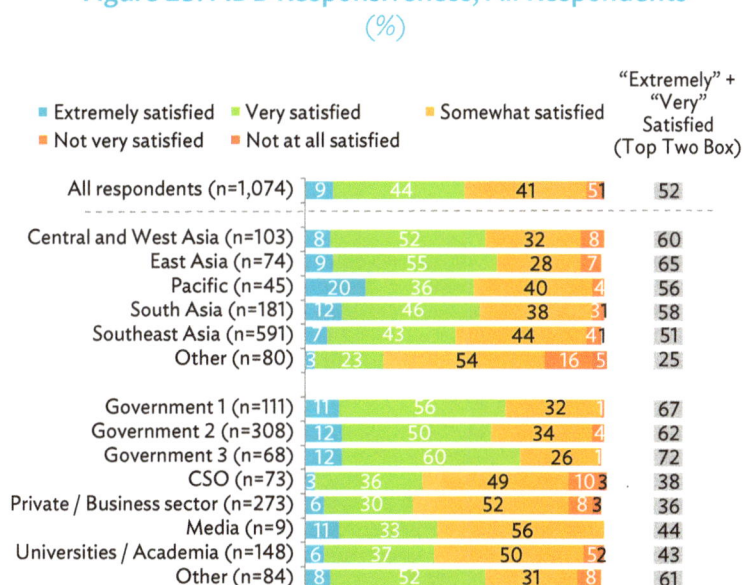

■ Extremely satisfied   ■ Very satisfied   ■ Somewhat satisfied
■ Not very satisfied   ■ Not at all satisfied

"Extremely" +
"Very"
Satisfied
(Top Two Box)

Respondent	Extremely satisfied	Very satisfied	Somewhat satisfied	Not very satisfied	Not at all satisfied	Top Two Box
All respondents (n=1,074)	9	44	41	5	1	52
Central and West Asia (n=103)	8	52	32	8		60
East Asia (n=74)	9	55	28	7		65
Pacific (n=45)	20	36	40	4		56
South Asia (n=181)	12	46	38	3	1	58
Southeast Asia (n=591)	7	43	44	4	1	51
Other (n=80)	3	23	54	16	5	25
Government 1 (n=111)	11	56	32	1		67
Government 2 (n=308)	12	50	34	4		62
Government 3 (n=68)	12	60	26	1		72
CSO (n=73)	3	36	49	10	3	38
Private / Business sector (n=273)	6	30	52	8	3	36
Media (n=9)	11	33	56			44
Universities / Academia (n=148)	6	37	50	5	2	43
Other (n=84)	8	52	31	8		61

ADB = Asian Development Bank, CSO = civil society organization, Government 1 = central government, Government 2 = line ministries, Government 3 = local governments, n = number of respondents.

Note: Survey base – entities familiar with ADB. "Other" pertains to respondents outside the listed group.

Source: Asian Development Bank Client Perceptions Survey 2020.

Figure 26: ADB Responsiveness, Primary Clients
(%)

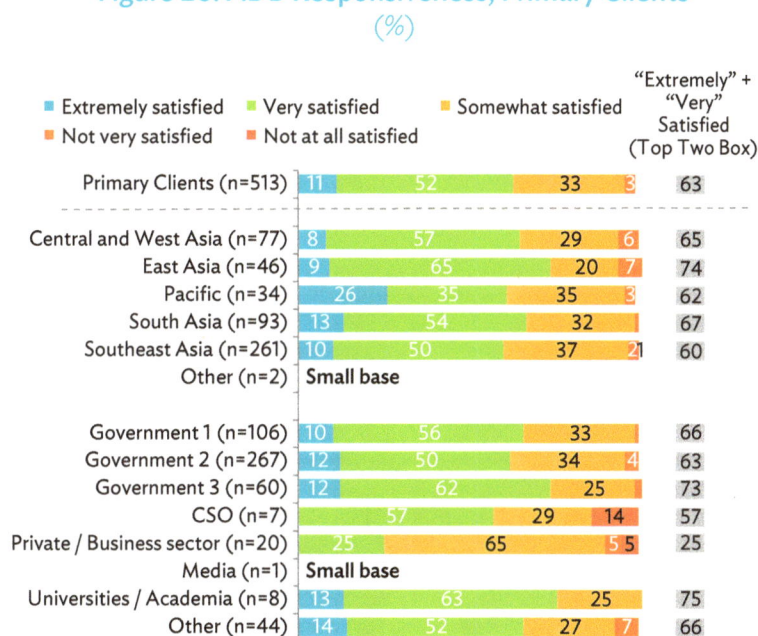

■ Extremely satisfied   ■ Very satisfied   ■ Somewhat satisfied
■ Not very satisfied   ■ Not at all satisfied

"Extremely" +
"Very"
Satisfied
(Top Two Box)

Respondent	Extremely satisfied	Very satisfied	Somewhat satisfied	Not very satisfied	Not at all satisfied	Top Two Box
Primary Clients (n=513)	11	52	33	3		63
Central and West Asia (n=77)	8	57	29	6		65
East Asia (n=46)	9	65	20	7		74
Pacific (n=34)	26	35	35	3		62
South Asia (n=93)	13	54	32	1		67
Southeast Asia (n=261)	10	50	37	2	1	60
Other (n=2)	Small base					
Government 1 (n=106)	10	56	33	1		66
Government 2 (n=267)	12	50	34	4		63
Government 3 (n=60)	12	62	25	1		73
CSO (n=7)		57	29	14		57
Private / Business sector (n=20)	25	65	5	5		25
Media (n=1)	Small base					
Universities / Academia (n=8)	13	63	25			75
Other (n=44)	14	52	27	7		66

ADB = Asian Development Bank, CSO = civil society organization, Government 1 = central government, Government 2 = line ministries, Government 3 = local governments, n = number of respondents.

Note: Survey base – entities familiar with ADB. Small base: n<5. "Other" pertains to respondents outside the listed group.

Source: Asian Development Bank Client Perceptions Survey 2020.

Figure 27: Top 12 Reasons Given for ADB's Overall Responsiveness Rating
(%)

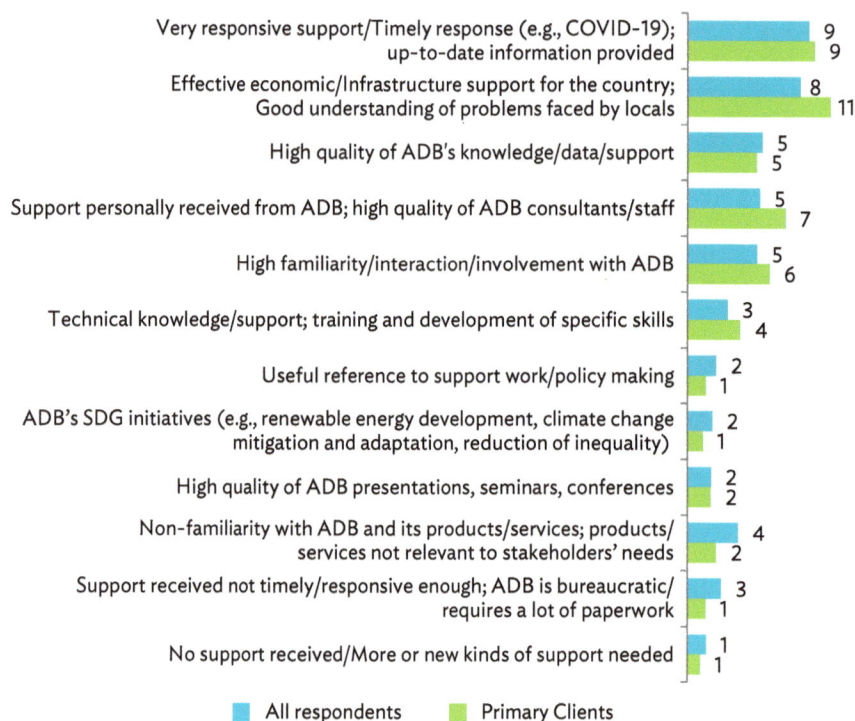

Reason	All respondents	Primary Clients
Very responsive support/Timely response (e.g., COVID-19); up-to-date information provided	9	9
Effective economic/Infrastructure support for the country; Good understanding of problems faced by locals	8	11
High quality of ADB's knowledge/data/support	5	5
Support personally received from ADB; high quality of ADB consultants/staff	5	7
High familiarity/interaction/involvement with ADB	5	6
Technical knowledge/support; training and development of specific skills	3	4
Useful reference to support work/policy making	2	1
ADB's SDG initiatives (e.g., renewable energy development, climate change mitigation and adaptation, reduction of inequality)	2	1
High quality of ADB presentations, seminars, conferences	2	2
Non-familiarity with ADB and its products/services; products/services not relevant to stakeholders' needs	4	2
Support received not timely/responsive enough; ADB is bureaucratic/requires a lot of paperwork	3	1
No support received/More or new kinds of support needed	1	1

ADB = Asian Development Bank, COVID-19 = coronavirus disease, SDG = Sustainable Development Goal.
Note: Survey base – entities familiar with ADB. All respondents = 1,074. Primary Clients = 513.
Source: Asian Development Bank Client Perceptions Survey 2020.

Collaboration with Development Partners

More than half of clients surveyed (54%, including those from "other" regions) say they are "extremely" or "very" satisfied with ADB's collaboration with its development partners, as shown in Figure 28.

Perceptions in this regard differ significantly between client groups. Clients in government organizations are more likely to be satisfied with ADB's collaboration with its development partners (62%–67%) than those working in the private sector

and CSOs, where the levels of satisfaction are quite low (39% and 36%, respectively).

Primary Clients, as Figure 29 shows, perceive ADB as collaborative with its development partners, with 63% saying they are "extremely" or "very" satisfied with the collaboration. The level of satisfaction across Asia and the Pacific ranges from 60% (South Asia) to 73% (East Asia).

The proportion of Primary Clients that are "extremely" or "very" satisfied varies widely between client groups. Satisfaction is highest among those in the university/academia sector (86%), and lowest among CSOs (43%) and the private/business sector (47%).

Figure 28: Collaboration with Development Partners, All Respondents
(%)

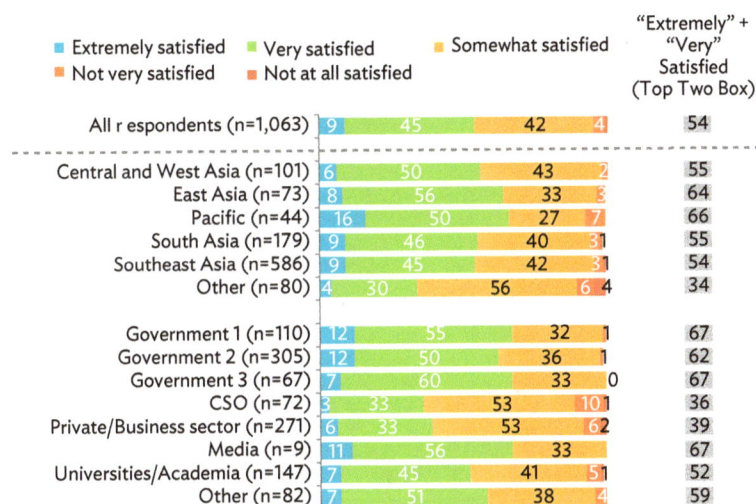

Legend: ■ Extremely satisfied ■ Very satisfied ■ Somewhat satisfied ■ Not very satisfied ■ Not at all satisfied

"Extremely" + "Very" Satisfied (Top Two Box)

Category	Extremely satisfied	Very satisfied	Somewhat satisfied	Not very satisfied	Not at all satisfied	Top Two Box
All respondents (n=1,063)	9	45	42	4		54
Central and West Asia (n=101)	6	50	43	2		55
East Asia (n=73)	8	56	33	3		64
Pacific (n=44)	16	50	27	7		66
South Asia (n=179)	9	46	40	3	1	55
Southeast Asia (n=586)	9	45	42	3	1	54
Other (n=80)	4	30	56	6	4	34
Government 1 (n=110)	12	55	32	1		67
Government 2 (n=305)	12	50	36	1		62
Government 3 (n=67)	7	60	33	0		67
CSO (n=72)	3	33	53	10	1	36
Private/Business sector (n=271)	6	33	53	6	2	39
Media (n=9)	11	56	33			67
Universities/Academia (n=147)	7	45	41	5	1	52
Other (n=82)	7	51	38	4		59

ADB = Asian Development Bank, CSO = civil society organization, Government 1 = central government, Government 2 = line ministries, Government 3 = local governments, n = number of respondents.

Note: Survey base – entities familiar with ADB. "Other" pertains to respondents outside the listed group.

Source: Asian Development Bank Client Perceptions Survey 2020.

Figure 29: Collaboration with Development Partners, Primary Clients
(%)

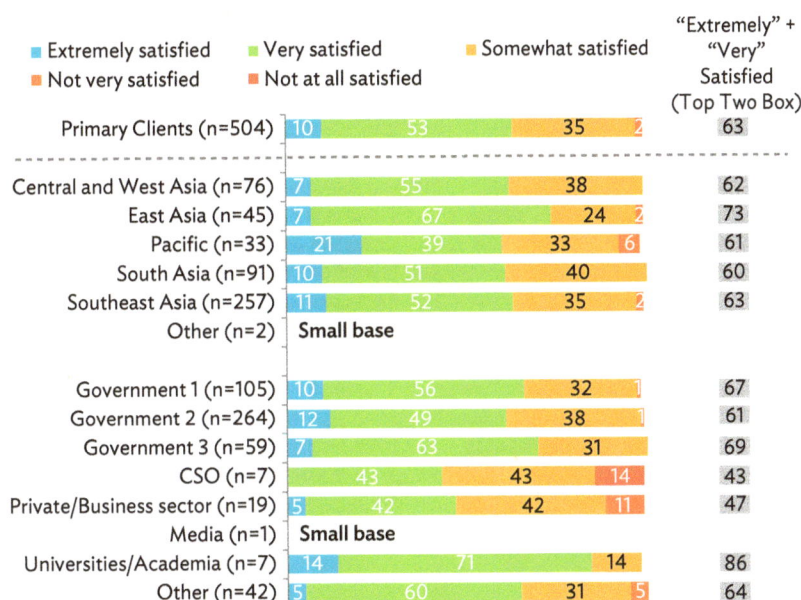

Legend: ■ Extremely satisfied ■ Very satisfied ■ Somewhat satisfied ■ Not very satisfied ■ Not at all satisfied

"Extremely" + "Very" Satisfied (Top Two Box)

Category	Extremely satisfied	Very satisfied	Somewhat satisfied	Not very satisfied	Not at all satisfied	Top Two Box
Primary Clients (n=504)	10	53	35	2		63
Central and West Asia (n=76)	7	55	38			62
East Asia (n=45)	7	67	24	2		73
Pacific (n=33)	21	39	33	6		61
South Asia (n=91)	10	51	40			60
Southeast Asia (n=257)	11	52	35	2		63
Other (n=2)	**Small base**					
Government 1 (n=105)	10	56	32	1		67
Government 2 (n=264)	12	49	38	1		61
Government 3 (n=59)	7	63	31			69
CSO (n=7)		43	43		14	43
Private/Business sector (n=19)	5	42	42	11		47
Media (n=1)	**Small base**					
Universities/Academia (n=7)	14	71	14			86
Other (n=42)	5	60	31	5		64

ADB = Asian Development Bank, CSO = civil society organization, Government 1 = central government, Government 2 = line ministries, Government 3 = local governments, n = number of respondents.

Note: Survey base – entities familiar with ADB. Small base: n<5; "Other" pertains to respondents outside the listed group.

Source: Asian Development Bank Client Perceptions Survey 2020.

Technical Assistance to DMCs

According to Figure 30, most respondents "strongly agree" or "agree" that ADB's technical assistance to DMCs aligns well with their country's development needs (78%), effectively addresses its knowledge needs (73%), and is efficiently provided (72%). These perceptions are more pronounced among Primary Clients, 83%–87% of which "strongly agree" or "agree" with these statements.

In all regions, these perceptions that ADB's technical assistance to its DMCs aligns well with their country's development needs, effectively addresses their knowledge needs, and is efficiently provided are stronger among Primary Clients than among all respondents.

Perceived Strengths

High level of satisfaction with ADB's development effectiveness at country level among Primary Clients

Primary Clients are satisfied overall with the help provided by ADB to their country in achieving development results (75% are "extremely" or "very" satisfied).

The high level of satisfaction is driven mostly by Primary Clients in government and the university/academia sector.

This factor represents ADB's greatest strength when it comes to its engagement at the country level, and indicates potential for ADB to build strong trust among Primary Clients.

Clients describe this strength as follows:

- "Overall, ADB listens to the country needs communicated by the government. It tailor-fits programs and technical assistance components to meet the pressing needs of the country."
  – Government client, Philippines

- "Prompt actions are taken according to the country's requirements" – CSO client, India

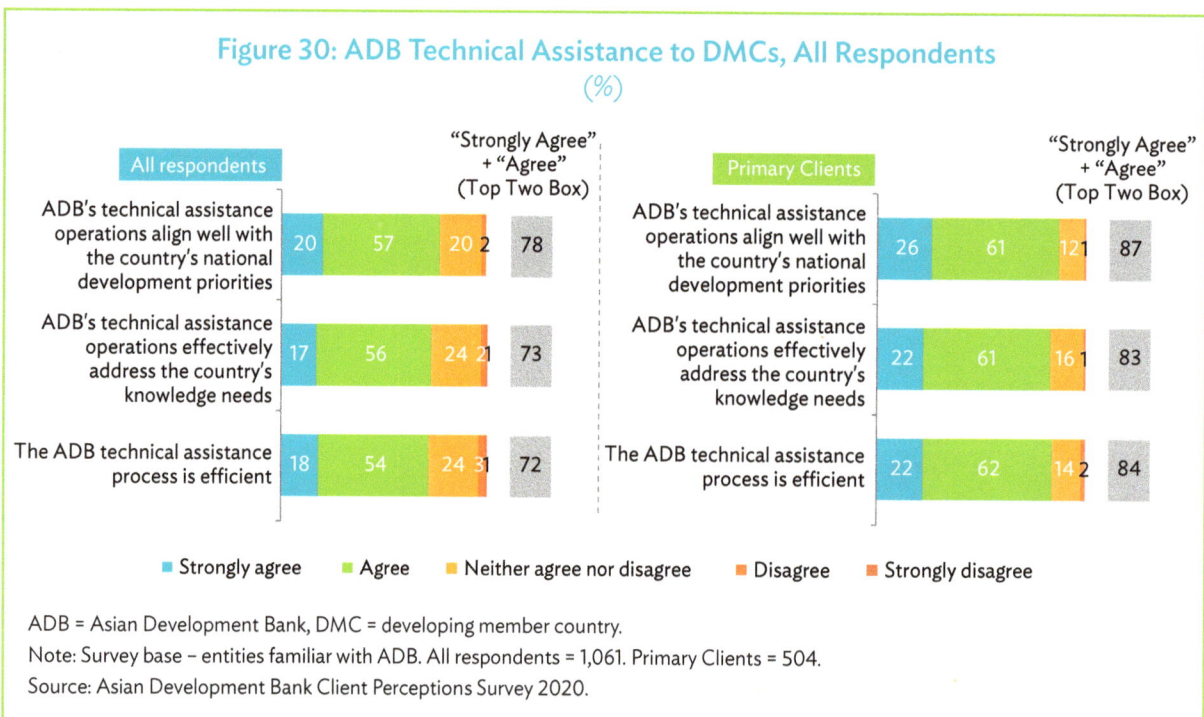

Figure 30: ADB Technical Assistance to DMCs, All Respondents (%)

All respondents

	"Strongly Agree" + "Agree" (Top Two Box)
ADB's technical assistance operations align well with the country's national development priorities	20 / 57 / 20 / 2 → **78**
ADB's technical assistance operations effectively address the country's knowledge needs	17 / 56 / 24 / 2 1 → **73**
The ADB technical assistance process is efficient	18 / 54 / 24 / 3 1 → **72**

Primary Clients

	"Strongly Agree" + "Agree" (Top Two Box)
ADB's technical assistance operations align well with the country's national development priorities	26 / 61 / 12 1 → **87**
ADB's technical assistance operations effectively address the country's knowledge needs	22 / 61 / 16 1 → **83**
The ADB technical assistance process is efficient	22 / 62 / 14 2 → **84**

■ Strongly agree ■ Agree ■ Neither agree nor disagree ■ Disagree ■ Strongly disagree

ADB = Asian Development Bank, DMC = developing member country.
Note: Survey base – entities familiar with ADB. All respondents = 1,061. Primary Clients = 504.
Source: Asian Development Bank Client Perceptions Survey 2020.

Improving infrastructure, promoting environmental sustainability, and strengthening governance and institutional capacity—ADB's highest-rated performance areas

Improving infrastructure is ADB's strongest performance area, according to Primary Clients (83%) as well as all clients surveyed (74%). The substantial help extended by ADB to countries to ease the transformation of developing cities therefore serves its purpose.

ADB clients share this view:

- "ADB has often been at the forefront of supporting fundamental policy change and enabling institutions to design and implement programs that are new to them. The critical role of ADB in development (especially in addressing infrastructure deficit, building capacity in institutions, developing skills) is very fundamental and is appreciated by policy makers, especially those in local and subregional governments, where local capacity to drive change is limited." – Private sector client, India

"Promoting environmental sustainability" is another major focus area of ADB, and its performance in this area is rated among its greatest strengths by clients. This high rating indicates the favorable reception from clients at the country level for ADB's integrated solutions, which combine expertise across a range of sectors and themes to achieve a prosperous, inclusive, resilient, and sustainable Asia and the Pacific.

ADB's clients, particularly its Primary Clients, also rate "strengthening governance and institutional capacity" among its chief assets, thus highlighting the vigorous efforts and commitment of ADB's Capacity Building and Training Department to strengthening the governance and institutional capacity of DMCs.

Areas for Improvement

Responsiveness

Clients across most regions and groups say that ADB performance is weakest in its responsiveness to their needs. This view is held by many clients in the private sector, CSOs, and universities/academia, where the level of satisfaction is relatively low (36%–43%).

The main drivers of the negative responsiveness ratings are "lack of familiarity with ADB" and ADB's "insufficient responsiveness," as reflected in statements made by some clients:

- "ADB staff and individuals are quite responsive, but as an organization, ADB is not as responsive." – Private sector client, People's Republic of China
- "I've encountered roadblocks in gaining access to staff in matters important to my work. It seems ADB has become more bureaucratic in recent years." – Private sector client, Philippines

Collaboration with Development Partners

Only slightly over half of the clients surveyed (54%) are satisfied with ADB's effectiveness in its collaboration with its various development partners. ADB's relationships with these partners can be strengthened further.

This is especially considered a weakness among clients working in the private sector and CSOs.

Clients from the private sector and CSOs describe what they perceive as the main weaknesses in ADB's collaboration with development partners:

- "I feel that there is still a lack of awareness of whom ADB deals with or coordinates with. Such information must be made more available to the public to give a better and clearer picture of just how far and wide ADB's support goes, and those it aids in developing and improving for the long term." – *Private sector client, Philippines*
- "More collaborative work, particularly with civil society organizations, is needed." – *CSO client, India*

8 Impact of ADB's COVID-19 Response

Familiarity with ADB's COVID-19 Response

Familiarity with ADB's COVID-19 response is relatively high among Primary Clients (63% are "very" or "moderately" familiar), as shown in Figure 31.

Primary Clients from the Pacific subregion claim that they are the most familiar with ADB's COVID-19 response in their country (76% are "very" or "moderately" familiar). In the other subregions, this familiarity ranges between 60% and 64%. Familiarity

is highest among Primary Clients in the Government 3 group and in CSOs (69% and 71%, respectively).

ADB's Performance in Minimizing Adverse Effects of COVID-19

Among Primary Clients that are "very" or "moderately" familiar with ADB's COVID-19 response, Figure 32 shows that almost all give at least a "satisfactory" rating to the support provided to their country.

Figure 31: Familiarity with ADB's COVID-19 Response, Primary Clients (%)

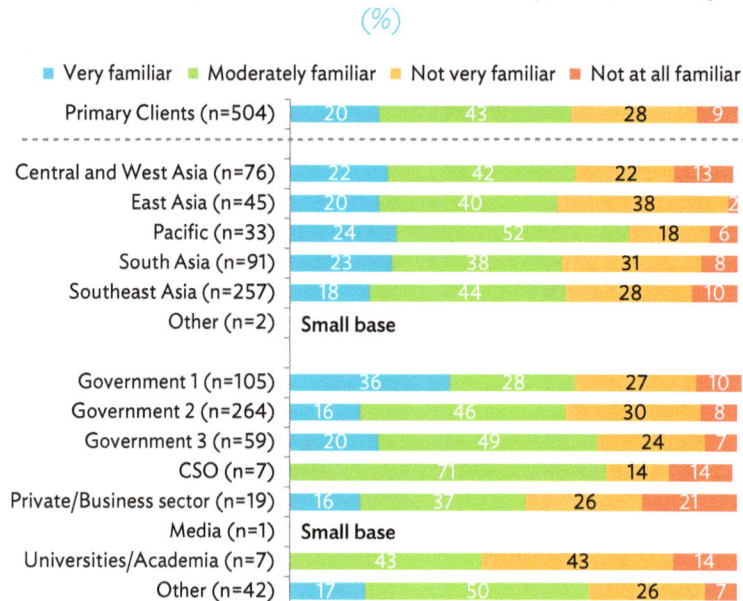

■ Very familiar ■ Moderately familiar ■ Not very familiar ■ Not at all familiar

	Very familiar	Moderately familiar	Not very familiar	Not at all familiar
Primary Clients (n=504)	20	43	28	9
Central and West Asia (n=76)	22	42	22	13
East Asia (n=45)	20	40	38	2
Pacific (n=33)	24	52	18	6
South Asia (n=91)	23	38	31	8
Southeast Asia (n=257)	18	44	28	10
Other (n=2)	Small base			
Government 1 (n=105)	36	28	27	10
Government 2 (n=264)	16	46	30	8
Government 3 (n=59)	20	49	24	7
CSO (n=7)		71	14	14
Private/Business sector (n=19)	16	37	26	21
Media (n=1)	Small base			
Universities/Academia (n=7)		43	43	14
Other (n=42)	17	50	26	7

ADB = Asian Development Bank, CSO = civil society organization, Government 1 = central government, Government 2 = line ministries, Government 3 = local governments, n = number of respondents.

Note: Survey base – Primary Clients familiar with ADB. Small base: n<5. "Other" pertains to respondents outside the listed group.

Source: Asian Development Bank Client Perceptions Survey 2020.

Figure 32: ADB's Performance in Minimizing Adverse Effects of COVID-19
(%)

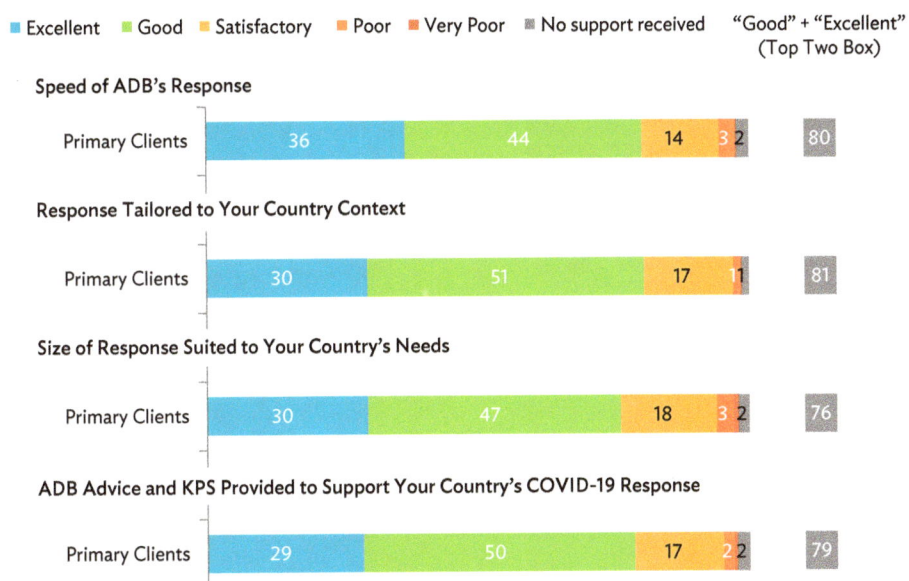

■ Excellent ■ Good ■ Satisfactory ■ Poor ■ Very Poor ■ No support received   "Good" + "Excellent"
(Top Two Box)

Speed of ADB's Response

Primary Clients | 36 | 44 | 14 | 3 | 2 | 80

Response Tailored to Your Country Context

Primary Clients | 30 | 51 | 17 | 1 | 1 | 81

Size of Response Suited to Your Country's Needs

Primary Clients | 30 | 47 | 18 | 3 | 2 | 76

ADB Advice and KPS Provided to Support Your Country's COVID-19 Response

Primary Clients | 29 | 50 | 17 | 2 | 2 | 79

ADB = Asian Development Bank, COVID-19 = coronavirus disease.

Note: Survey base – Primary Clients familiar with ADB and "very"/"moderately" familiar with ADB's COVID-19 response in their country. The base excludes Primary Clients that are "not very familiar" or "not at all familiar" with ADB's COVID-19 response. Primary Clients = 318

Source: Asian Development Bank Client Perceptions Survey 2020.

Eighty percent rate the speed of ADB's response "good" or "excellent," and 81% believe that ADB tailors its response to their country context.

Primary Clients generally accord positive ratings to the extent of ADB's COVID-19 support in relation to their country's needs. But there are differences between subregions: Primary Clients in the Pacific and Southeast Asia subregions tend to give the highest ratings, while those in East Asia give more average ratings.

Results Achieved by ADB in Addressing COVID-19

Figure 33 shows that among Primary Clients that are "very" or "moderately" familiar with ADB's COVID-19 response in their country, the impact made by that response gets a positive rating (88% find the results achieved "satisfactory" or better; 73% rate those results "excellent" or "good").

The Pacific and Southeast Asia are the subregions where most of the results achieved have been observed, and these are also the regions where the ADB response has had the most positive impact: four in ten Primary Clients in the Pacific subregion that are "very" or "moderately" familiar with ADB's COVID-19 response (40%) give the results an "excellent" rating.

Among Primary Clients that are "very"/"moderately" familiar with ADB's COVID-19 response in their country, 89% find the results achieved by ADB in addressing COVID-19 "excellent," "good," or "satisfactory."

Figure 33: Results Achieved by ADB in Addressing COVID-19, Primary Clients (%)

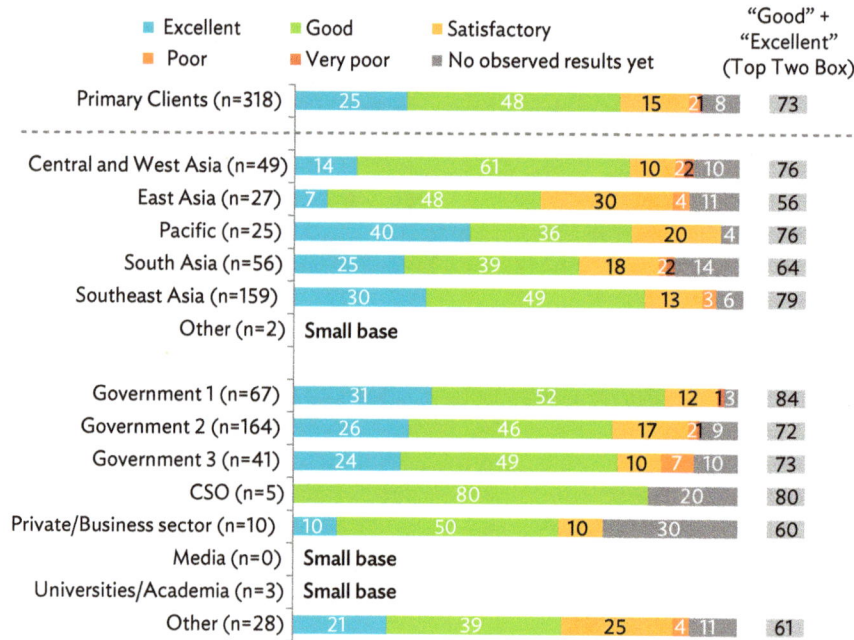

Legend: Excellent, Good, Satisfactory, Poor, Very poor, No observed results yet

	Excellent	Good	Satisfactory	Poor	Very poor	No observed results yet	"Good" + "Excellent" (Top Two Box)
Primary Clients (n=318)	25	48	15	2	1	8	73
Central and West Asia (n=49)	14	61	10	2	2	10	76
East Asia (n=27)	7	48	30	4		11	56
Pacific (n=25)	40	36	20			4	76
South Asia (n=56)	25	39	18	2	2	14	64
Southeast Asia (n=159)	30	49	13	3		6	79
Other (n=2)	Small base						
Government 1 (n=67)	31	52	12	1		3	84
Government 2 (n=164)	26	46	17	2	1	9	72
Government 3 (n=41)	24	49	10	7		10	73
CSO (n=5)		80				20	80
Private/Business sector (n=10)	10	50	10			30	60
Media (n=0)	Small base						
Universities/Academia (n=3)	Small base						
Other (n=28)	21	39	25	4		11	61

ADB = Asian Development Bank, COVID-19= coronavirus disease, CSO = civil society organization, Government 1 = central government, Government 2 = line ministries, Government 3 = local governments, n = number of respondents.

Note: Survey base – Primary Clients familiar with ADB and "very"/"moderately" familiar with ADB's COVID-19 response in their country. The base excludes Primary Clients that are "not very familiar" or "not at all familiar" with ADB's COVID-19 response. Small base: n<5. "Other" pertains to respondents outside the listed group.

Source: Asian Development Bank Client Perceptions Survey 2020.

Excluding "No Observed Results Yet"

Among Primary Clients that have seen results from ADB's COVID-19 response in their country, the vast majority agree that ADB's support has had some positive impact.

The impact has been most significant in the Pacific subregion, where 96% of all Primary Clients with some familiarity with ADB's COVID-19 response consider the results achieved at least "satisfactory," and 40% rate the results "excellent."

The positive impact has been felt most strongly by Primary Clients in the Government 1 group and CSOs, among the client groups (83% of Primary Clients in the first group and 80% in the second group rate the results "excellent" or "good").

Among Primary Clients who are moderately/very familiar with ADB's COVID-19 response in their country and excluding the ones who had not yet observed the results, between 83% and 95% of those working in government organizations give the results achieved a rating of at least "satisfactory."

Perceptions of ADB's Evaluation Knowledge

Familiarity

One-third of all clients surveyed (36%) say they are "very" or "moderately" familiar with ADB's evaluation KPS. Primary Clients have a similar level of familiarity. Both groups of respondents are mostly familiar with evaluation reports and recommendations, and least familiar with the Asian Evaluation Week

Within Asia and the Pacific, the level of familiarity with the various KPS ranges between 34% and 44%. Clients from "other" regions (45% are "not familiar at all") account for the relatively low familiarity overall.

Clients in government organizations, particularly those from the Government 2 and 3 groups, are the most familiar with ADB's evaluation KPS (44% and 48%, respectively, claim that they are "very" or "moderately" familiar). Familiarity is lowest among CSO and private sector clients.

Importance

A majority of all respondents (65%), particularly those working in government and in the Pacific subregion, agree that ADB's evaluation KPS are important sources of learning, as shown in Figure 34.

Figure 34: Importance of ADB's Evaluation KPS as Sources of Learning, All Respondents Familiar with These KPS
(%)

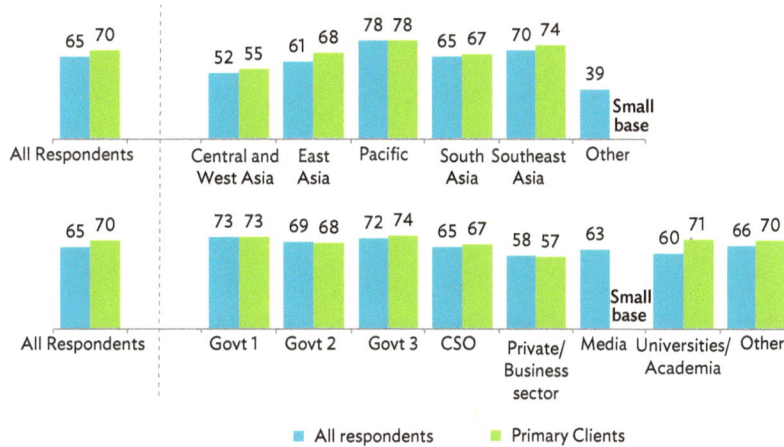

ADB = Asian Development Bank, CSO = civil society organization, Govt 1 = Government 1 (central government), Govt 2 = Government 2 (line ministries), Govt 3 = Government 3 (local governments), KPS = knowledge products and services.

Note: Survey base – entities familiar ("very," "moderately," or "not very" familiar) with ADB's independent evaluation knowledge products and services (77% of all respondents). The base excludes those that are "not very familiar" or "not at all familiar" with those knowledge products and services. All respondents = 853. Primary Clients = 434. Small base: n<5. "Other" pertains to respondents outside the listed group.

Source: Asian Development Bank Client Perceptions Survey 2020.

Primary Clients are slightly more likely (70%) to share that view. The higher importance rating is driven mostly by Primary Clients in the Pacific subregion (78%) and Southeast Asia (74%).

Usage

Clients mostly use ADB's evaluation KPS to deepen their understanding of development issues and to guide them in designing new policies, strategies, programs, and projects.

Figure 35 shows that 63% of all clients and 66% of Primary Clients say they mostly use ADB's evaluation knowledge products when they want to deepen their understanding of development issues.

However, there is a significant gap between Primary Clients (63%) and all clients (53%) in the use of ADB's evaluation KPS in designing new policies, strategies, programs, and projects.

With one in three clients using these KPS to bring about helpful change, there is room to further showcase these KPS and promote such use.

Figure 35: Use of ADB's Evaluation Knowledge Products, Respondents
(%)

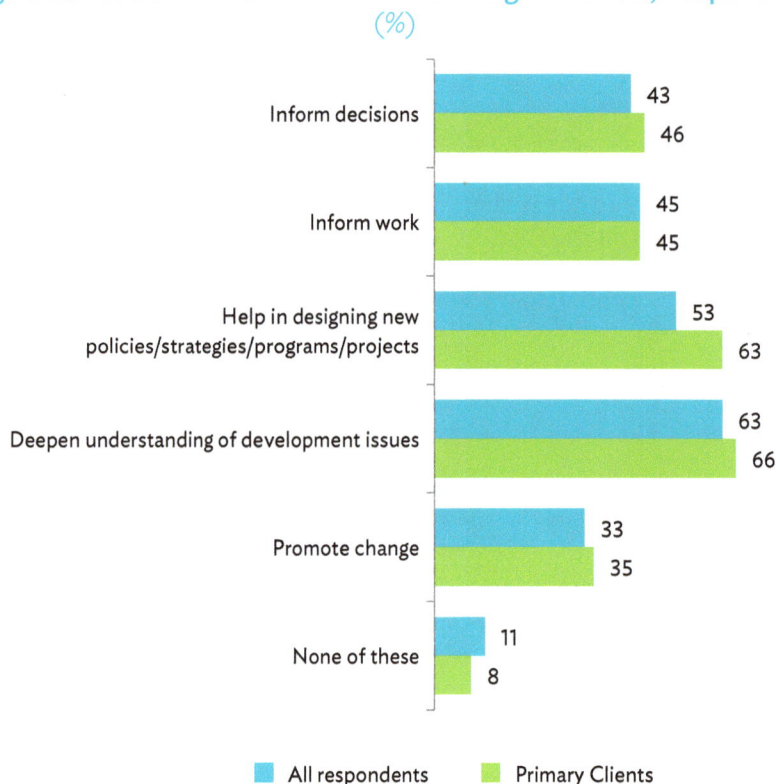

Category	All respondents	Primary Clients
Inform decisions	43	46
Inform work	45	45
Help in designing new policies/strategies/programs/projects	53	63
Deepen understanding of development issues	63	66
Promote change	33	35
None of these	11	8

■ All respondents   ■ Primary Clients

ADB = Asian Development Bank.

Note: Survey base – entities familiar ("very," "moderately," or "not very" familiar) with ADB's independent evaluation knowledge products and services. The base excludes those that are "not very familiar" or "not at all familiar" with those knowledge products and services. All respondents = 846. Primary Clients = 432.

Source: Asian Development Bank Client Perceptions Survey 2020.

Usefulness

The majority of the clients surveyed consider these "extremely," "very," or "somewhat" useful, as can be seen in Figure 36.

The ADB evaluation knowledge products and services that are deemed most useful by clients are evaluation reports (64% "extremely" or "very" useful), evaluation recommendations (62%), and evaluation workshops and training (61%). These same products are rated most useful by Primary Clients.

Overall, ADB's evaluation KPS are slightly more useful to Primary Clients than to all respondents.

The Asian Evaluation Week gets the lowest usefulness ratings, with less than half of clients (40%) finding it "extremely" or "very" useful.

The level of familiarity with the different ADB evaluation KPS is similar among all respondents and among Primary Clients. They are mostly familiar with evaluation reports and evaluation recommendations, and least familiar with the Asian Evaluation Week. Among clients familiar with ADB's evaluation KPS, the vast majority find these products and services "extremely," "very," or "somewhat" useful.

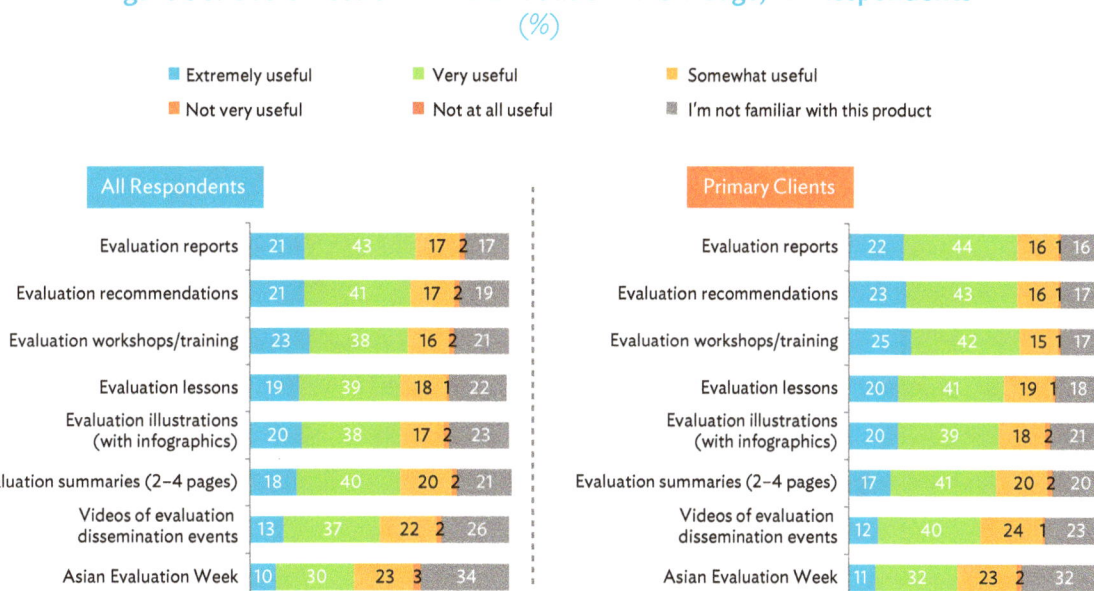

Figure 36: Usefulness of ADB's Evaluation Knowledge, All Respondents (%)

ADB = Asian Development Bank, KPS = knowledge products and services.

Note: Survey base – entities familiar ("very," "moderately," or "not very" familiar) with ADB's independent evaluation knowledge products and services. The base excludes those that are "not very familiar" or "not at all familiar" with those knowledge products and services. All respondents = 847. Primary Clients = 433.

Source: Asian Development Bank Client Perceptions Survey 2020.

10 Income, FCAS, and SIDS Classification of Countries

ADB Knowledge Products, Services, and Events

Familiarity

Familiarity with ADB KPS among all clients as well as Primary Clients is highest in low-income countries (LICs)[4] and in fragile and conflict-affected states (FCAS).[5] Familiarity with ADB KPS among small island developing states (SIDS),[6] where close to four in ten clients are "not very" familiar, according to Figure 37, can and should be increased.

Usage and Usefulness

Tables 5 and 6 show that webinars, seminars, workshops, and conferences, as well as books, technical studies, reports, and working papers, are among the most used KPS in all country groups. Capacity building / Training is highly used in FCAS and SIDS, and also in LICs.

Capacity building / Training and books, technical studies, reports, and working papers are perceived as the most useful ADB KPS in low-income countries (LICs), lower middle-income countries (LMICs), and upper middle-income countries (UMICs). Multimedia events are also considered highly useful in UMICs, while policy dialogue and related activities are among the most useful KPS in FCAS and SIDS.

Almost all Primary Clients in LICs, LMICs, and UMICs regard capacity building / training as useful in their work (Table 8). It is also worth noting that multimedia events are among the most useful ADB KPS for Primary Clients in FCAS and SIDS, as shown in Table 6.

---

[4] ADB has adopted the World Bank system of country classification by income for its DMCs. The World Bank updates each year the range of gross national income (GNI) per capita that determines a country's income classification. World Bank. 2021. https://datahelpdesk.worldbank.org/knowledgebase/articles/906519.

[5] ADB classifies 11 countries as fragile and conflict-affected states (FCAS). The classification is based on an assessment of the quality of macroeconomic management, the coherence of structural policies, the degree to which policies and institutions promote equity and inclusion, the quality of governance and public sector management, and the performance of the concessional assistance project portfolio. FCAS DMCs are generally characterized by political instability, weak governance and institutional capacity, economic and social insecurity, and greater vulnerability to the effects of climate change and natural hazards. Asian Development Bank. 2021. https://www.adb.org/fcas-sids-approach.

[6] Small island developing states (SIDS) are a distinct group of 16 countries with specific social, economic, and environmental vulnerabilities, including geographic remoteness and dispersion, small populations and markets, narrow-based economies, low fiscal revenue, high import and export costs of goods, and increasing exposure to natural hazards and climate change. SIDS in Asia and the Pacific are affected by extreme fragility, which can threaten lives and livelihoods, strain state capacity and service provision, and heighten local tensions over scarce land and other resources. Asian Development Bank. 2021. https://www.adb.org/fcas-sids-approach.

Figure 37: Familiarity with ADB KPS, All Respondents
(%)

■ Very familiar   ■ Moderately familiar   ■ Not very familiar   ■ Not familiar at all

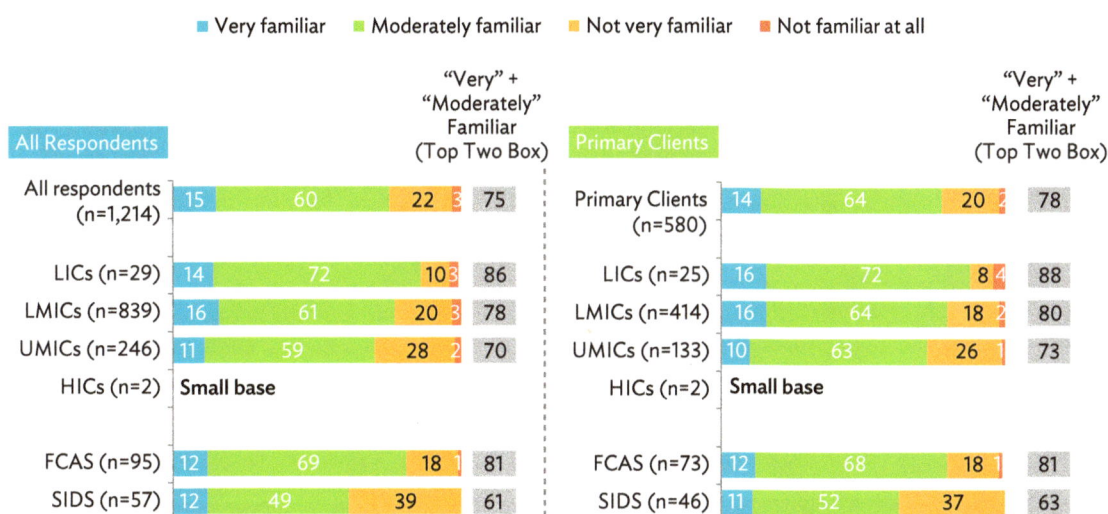

All Respondents — "Very" + "Moderately" Familiar (Top Two Box)

	Very	Moderately	Not very	Not at all	Top Two Box
All respondents (n=1,214)	15	60	22	3	75
LICs (n=29)	14	72	10	3	86
LMICs (n=839)	16	61	20	3	78
UMICs (n=246)	11	59	28	2	70
HICs (n=2)	Small base				
FCAS (n=95)	12	69	18	1	81
SIDS (n=57)	12	49	39		61

Primary Clients — "Very" + "Moderately" Familiar (Top Two Box)

	Very	Moderately	Not very	Not at all	Top Two Box
Primary Clients (n=580)	14	64	20	2	78
LICs (n=25)	16	72	8	4	88
LMICs (n=414)	16	64	18	2	80
UMICs (n=133)	10	63	26	1	73
HICs (n=2)	Small base				
FCAS (n=73)	12	68	18	1	81
SIDS (n=46)	11	52	37		63

ADB = Asian Development Bank, FCAS = fragile and conflict-affected state, HIC = high-income country, KPS = knowledge products and services, LIC = low-income country, LMIC = lower middle-income country, n = number of respondents, SIDS = small island developing state, UMIC = upper middle-income country.

Note: Survey base – entities familiar with ADB. Small base: n<5. "Other" pertains to respondents outside the listed group.

Source: Asian Development Bank Client Perceptions Survey 2020.

Table 5: Use of ADB KPS at Work, All Respondents
(%)

ADB Knowledge Product/Service	All Respondents	By Income				By Situation	
		LICs	LMICs	UMICs	HICs	FCAS	SIDS
	n=1,178	n=28	n=815	n=240	n=2	n=94	n=57
Webinars/Seminars/Workshops/Conferences	75	71	76	71	Small base	59	70
Books / Technical studies / Reports / Working papers	58	50	57	60		52	54
Short reports (policy briefs, blogs, op-eds, etc.)	47	46	46	46		38	39
Capacity building / Training	45	57	47	45		62	61
Process/Project management / Technical capacity development	34	43	36	33		45	46
Policy dialogue and related activities	32	32	31	36		27	33
Multimedia (podcasts, videos, infographics, PowerPoint presentations, etc.)	31	25	31	30		30	46

ADB = Asian Development Bank, FCAS = fragile and conflict-affected state, HIC = high-income country, KPS = knowledge products and services, LIC = low-income country, LMIC = lower middle-income country, n = number of respondents, SIDS = small island developing state, UMIC = upper middle-income country.

Note: Survey base – entities familiar with ADB knowledge products, services, and events. Small base: n<5. Green cells highlight the top-3 scores for each group.

Source: Asian Development Bank Client Perceptions Survey 2020.

Table 6: Use of ADB KPS at Work, Primary Clients
(%)

ADB Knowledge Product/Service	Primary Clients	By Income				By Situation	
		LICs	LMICs	UMICs	HICs	FCAS	SIDS
	n=570	n=24	n=406	n=132	n=2	n=72	n=46
Webinars/Seminars/Workshops/Conferences	70	71	71	67		58	70
Books / Technical studies / Reports / Working papers	51	50	50	54		50	54
Short reports (policy briefs, blogs, op-eds, etc.)	41	42	40	39		39	41
Capacity building / Training	63	67	64	58	Small base	72	72
Process/Project management / Technical capacity development	46	50	47	42		53	50
Policy dialogue and related activities	34	38	33	39		29	35
Multimedia (podcasts, videos, infographics, PowerPoint presentations, etc.)	28	21	28	28		28	43

ADB = Asian Development Bank, FCAS = fragile and conflict-affected state, HIC = high-income country, KPS = knowledge products and services, LIC = low-income country, LMIC = lower middle-income country, n = number of respondents, SIDS = small island developing state, UMIC = upper middle-income country.

Note: Survey base – entities familiar with ADB knowledge products, services, and events. Small base: n<5. Green cells highlight the top-3 scores for each group.

Source: Asian Development Bank Client Perceptions Survey 2020.

Table 7: Usefulness of ADB KPS at Work, All Respondents
(%)

ADB Knowledge Product/Service	All Respondents	By Income				By Situation	
		LICs	LMICs	UMICs	HICs	FCAS	SIDS
Capacity building / Training (n=533)	89	94	90	89		86	97
Books / Technical studies / Reports / Working papers (n=683)	88	93	90	86		86	90
Process/Project management / Technical capacity development (n=404)	87	92	88	85	Small base	90	96
Webinars/Seminars/Workshops/Conferences (n=881)	84	85	87	78		85	85
Policy dialogue and related activities (n=379)	83	89	86	79		88	95
Short reports (n=557)	81	77	84	82		75	91
Multimedia events (n=369)	80	71	81	86		79	88

ADB = Asian Development Bank, FCAS = fragile and conflict-affected state, HIC = high-income country, KPS = knowledge products and services, LIC = low-income country, LMIC = lower middle-income country, n = number of respondents, SIDS = small island developing state, UMIC = upper middle-income country.

Note: Survey base – users of the knowledge product, service, or event (base indicated by product for all respondents). Small base: n<5. Green cells highlight the top-3 scores for each group.

Source: Asian Development Bank Client Perceptions Survey 2020.

Table 8: Usefulness of ADB KPS at Work, Primary Clients
(%)

ADB Knowledge Product/Service	Primary Clients	By Income				By Situation	
		LICs	LMICs	UMICs	HICs	FCAS	SIDS
Capacity building / Training (n=358)	93	94	92	96		88	100
Books / Technical studies / reports / Working papers (n=292)	91	100	92	86		89	92
Processes/Project management / Technical capacity development (n=265)	90	92	91	86	Small base	89	96
Webinars/Seminars/Workshops/Conferences (n=399)	87	82	90	79		86	88
Policy dialogue and related activities (n=196)	88	89	90	80		90	94
Short reports (n=231)	83	80	83	81		79	89
Multimedia events (n=160)	85	60	85	86		90	95

ADB = Asian Development Bank, FCAS = fragile and conflict-affected state, HIC = high-income country, KPS = knowledge products and services, LIC = low-income country, LMIC = lower middle-income country, n = number of respondents, SIDS = small island developing state, UMIC = upper middle-income country.

Note: Survey base – users of the knowledge product, service, or event (base indicated by product for all respondents). Small base: n<5. Green cells highlight the top-3 scores for each group.

Source: Asian Development Bank Client Perceptions Survey 2020.

In LICs, LMICs, and UMICs, ADB KPS are considered most useful in designing and implementing policies, programs, and projects. The usefulness of self-education can and should be showcased in LICs to increase its use.

ADB KPS are deemed highly useful by clients in SIDS, particularly when it comes to designing and implementing policies, programs, and projects. Clients in FCAS perceive ADB KPS as less useful in their work overall than those working in SIDS.

Overall Usefulness

Figure 38 shows that ADB KPS are considered highly useful among clients in SIDS: nine in ten rate ADB KPS "extremely" or "very" useful. When looking at the different income groups of countries, the clients, and particularly Primary Clients, who work in LMICs give the highest usefulness ratings to ADB KPs.

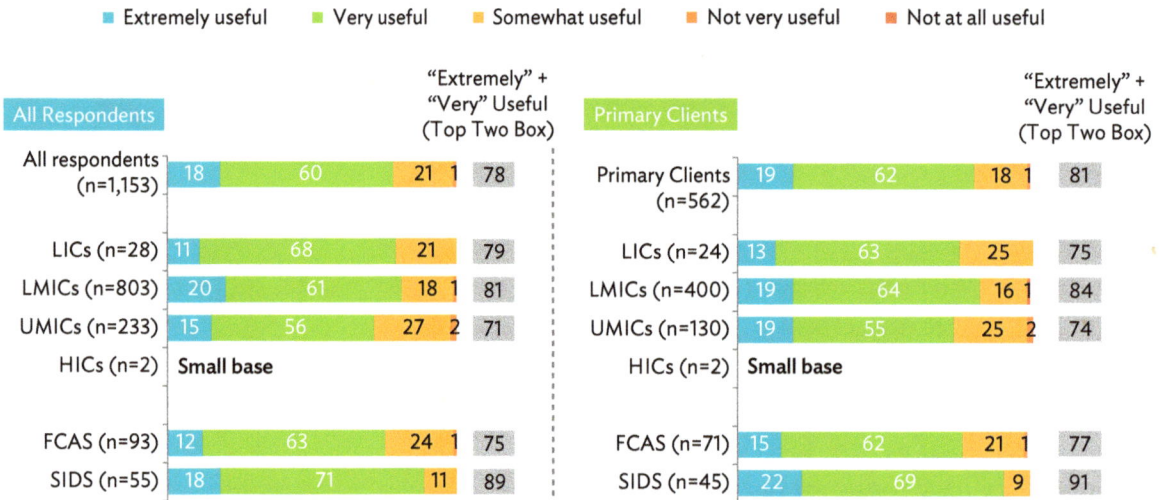

Figure 38: Overall Usefulness of ADB KPS, All Respondents
(%)

■ Extremely useful ■ Very useful ■ Somewhat useful ■ Not very useful ■ Not at all useful

All Respondents	Extremely useful	Very useful	Somewhat useful	Not very useful	"Extremely" + "Very" Useful (Top Two Box)
All respondents (n=1,153)	18	60	21	1	78
LICs (n=28)	11	68	21		79
LMICs (n=803)	20	61	18	1	81
UMICs (n=233)	15	56	27	2	71
HICs (n=2)	Small base				
FCAS (n=93)	12	63	24	1	75
SIDS (n=55)	18	71	11		89

Primary Clients	Extremely useful	Very useful	Somewhat useful	Not very useful	"Extremely" + "Very" Useful (Top Two Box)
Primary Clients (n=562)	19	62	18	1	81
LICs (n=24)	13	63	25		75
LMICs (n=400)	19	64	16	1	84
UMICs (n=130)	19	55	25	2	74
HICs (n=2)	Small base				
FCAS (n=71)	15	62	21	1	77
SIDS (n=45)	22	69	9		91

ADB = Asian Development Bank, FCAS = fragile and conflict-affected state, HIC = high-income country, KPS = knowledge products, and services, LIC = low-income country, LMIC = lower middle-income country, n = number of respondents, SIDS = small island developing state, UMIC = upper middle-income country.

Note: Survey base – entities familiar with ADB knowledge products, services, and events. Small base: n<5. "Other" pertains to respondents outside the listed group.

Source: Asian Development Bank Client Perceptions Survey 2020.

Timeliness

The majority of clients surveyed (66%) agree that ADB KPS are delivered in a timely manner, particularly clients working in LMICs and SIDS.

All respondents and Primary Clients in LMICs give the highest ratings to the timeliness of ADB KPS delivery. Those working in LICs give the lowest ratings.

The main gap in timeliness is found among those working in FCAS, where 80% of Primary Clients rate the delivery of ADB KPS "excellent" or "good," compared with 54% of all respondents.

Benefits

The "increased knowledge from capacity building / training courses" is perceived as the top benefit gained from using ADB KPS in LMICs, FCAS, and SIDS; while the top benefit among all clients working in LICs and UMICs is the "improved project design and implementation," as shown in Table 9.

Among Primary Clients, Table 10 indicates that the "increased knowledge from capacity building and training courses" and 'improved project design and implementation' are top benefits among all income groups.

Table 9: Benefits of ADB KPS, All Respondents
(% Ranking Each Benefit among the Top Three)

Benefit	All Respondents	By Income				By Situation	
		LICs	LMICs	UMICs	HICs	FCAS	SIDS
	n=904	n=22	n=642	n=179	n=2	n=69	n=48
Access to data and information in policy documents, reports, and articles	28	18	28	25	Small base	25	15
Increased knowledge from capacity building and training courses	27	23	30	24		36	35
Improved project design and implementation	27	45	26	28		35	35
Clearer understanding of policy issues and implications	25	18	25	27		17	23
New innovation ideas	23	32	22	26		14	27
Better decision-making	17	14	18	14		26	19
Access to knowledge useful in implementing climate change–related actions	16	18	15	19		12	8
Access to high-quality research	16	5	17	16		13	21

ADB = Asian Development Bank, FCAS = fragile and conflict-affected state, HIC = high-income country, KPS = knowledge products and services, LIC = low-income country, LMIC = lower middle-income country, n = number of respondents, SIDS = small island developing state, UMIC = upper middle-income country.

Note: Survey base – users of at least one ADB KPS in survey question Q2. Small base: n<5. Green cells highlight the top-3 scores for each group.

Source: Asian Development Bank Client Perceptions Survey 2020.

Table 10: Benefits Gained from Using ADB KPS, Primary Clients
(% Ranking Each Benefit among the Top Three)

Benefit	Primary Clients	By Income				By Situation	
		LICs	LMICs	UMICs	HICs	FCAS	SIDS
	n=459	n=21	n=328	n=104	n=2	n=54	n=39
Increased knowledge from capacity building and training courses	39	24	42	33	Small base	39	41
Improved project design and implementation	32	48	30	35		41	36
Clearer understanding of policy issues and implications	23	19	22	28		17	23
Better decision making	20	14	21	16		28	23
New innovation ideas	20	29	17	28		13	26
Access to data and information useful in preparing policies, reports, and articles	19	19	20	16		22	10
Help in formulating policies	18	10	19	18		15	5
Familiarity with procurement and monitoring tools	17	24	19	7		15	23

ADB = Asian Development Bank, FCAS = fragile and conflict-affected state, HIC = high-income country, KPS = knowledge products and services, LIC = low-income country, LMIC = lower middle-income country, n = number of respondents, SIDS = small island developing state, UMIC = upper middle-income country.

Note: Survey base – users of at least one ADB KPS in survey question Q2. Small base: n<5. Green cells highlight the top-3 scores for each group.

Source: Asian Development Bank Client Perceptions Survey 2020.

ADB's Development and Organizational Effectiveness

Development Effectiveness

As shown in Figure 39, the level of satisfaction with ADB's development effectiveness is higher overall among Primary Clients than among all respondents. It is highest among LICs and SIDS; eight in ten are "extremely" or "very" satisfied.

Responsiveness

The level of satisfaction with ADB's responsiveness across all country groups indicates that ADB has much room to improve in this area. In most country groups, only a little over half of all the clients surveyed are "extremely" or "very" satisfied with ADB's responsiveness. Clients in FCAS are the least satisfied with ADB's responsiveness, as shown in Figure 40.

ADB's Collaboration with Development Partners

According to Figure 41, only slightly over half of all clients surveyed (54%) and two in three Primary Clients (63%) are satisfied with ADB's collaboration with its various development partners. Clients in FCAS are the least satisfied. ADB has a significant opportunity to further strengthen its collaboration with these partners to build synergy.

Figure 39: ADB's Development Effectiveness, All Respondents
(%)

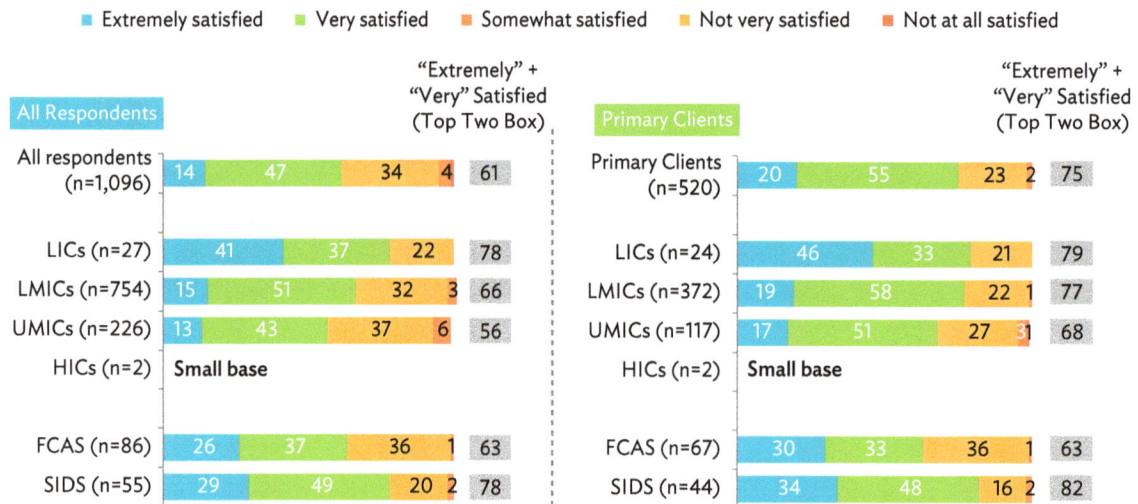

Legend: ■ Extremely satisfied ■ Very satisfied ■ Somewhat satisfied ■ Not very satisfied ■ Not at all satisfied

All Respondents — "Extremely" + "Very" Satisfied (Top Two Box)

Group	Extremely	Very	Somewhat	Not very	Not at all	Top Two Box
All respondents (n=1,096)	14	47	34	4		61
LICs (n=27)	41	37	22			78
LMICs (n=754)	15	51	32	3		66
UMICs (n=226)	13	43	37	6		56
HICs (n=2)	Small base					
FCAS (n=86)	26	37	36	1		63
SIDS (n=55)	29	49	20	2		78

Primary Clients — "Extremely" + "Very" Satisfied (Top Two Box)

Group	Extremely	Very	Somewhat	Not very	Not at all	Top Two Box
Primary Clients (n=520)	20	55	23	2		75
LICs (n=24)	46	33	21			79
LMICs (n=372)	19	58	22	1		77
UMICs (n=117)	17	51	27	3	1	68
HICs (n=2)	Small base					
FCAS (n=67)	30	33	36	1		63
SIDS (n=44)	34	48	16	2		82

ADB = Asian Development Bank, FCAS = fragile and conflict-affected state, HIC = high-income country LIC = low-income country, LMIC = lower middle-income country, n = number of respondents, SIDS = small island developing state, UMIC = upper middle-income countries.
Note: Survey base – entities familiar with ADB. Small base: n<5.
Source: Asian Development Bank Client Perceptions Survey 2020.

Figure 40: ADB's Responsiveness, All Respondents
(%)

■ Extremely satisfied ■ Very satisfied ■ Somewhat satisfied ■ Not very satisfied ■ Not at all satisfied

All Respondents		"Extremely" + "Very" Satisfied (Top Two Box)
All respondents (n=1,074)	9 / 44 / 41 / 5 / 1	52
LICs (n=26)	12 / 46 / 35 / 8	58
LMICs (n=742)	8 / 47 / 40 / 4 / 1	55
UMICs (n=221)	10 / 41 / 41 / 7 / 1	51
HICs (n=2)	Small base	
FCAS (n=86)	9 / 37 / 48 / 6	47
SIDS (n=54)	17 / 37 / 41 / 6	54

Primary Clients		"Extremely" + "Very" Satisfied (Top Two Box)
Primary Clients (n=513)	11 / 52 / 33 / 3	63
LICs (n=23)	13 / 52 / 26 / 9	65
LMICs (n=368)	10 / 54 / 34 / 2	64
UMICs (n=115)	15 / 48 / 32 / 5	63
HICs (n=2)	Small base	
FCAS (n=67)	12 / 37 / 43 / 7	49
SIDS (n=43)	21 / 37 / 37 / 5	58

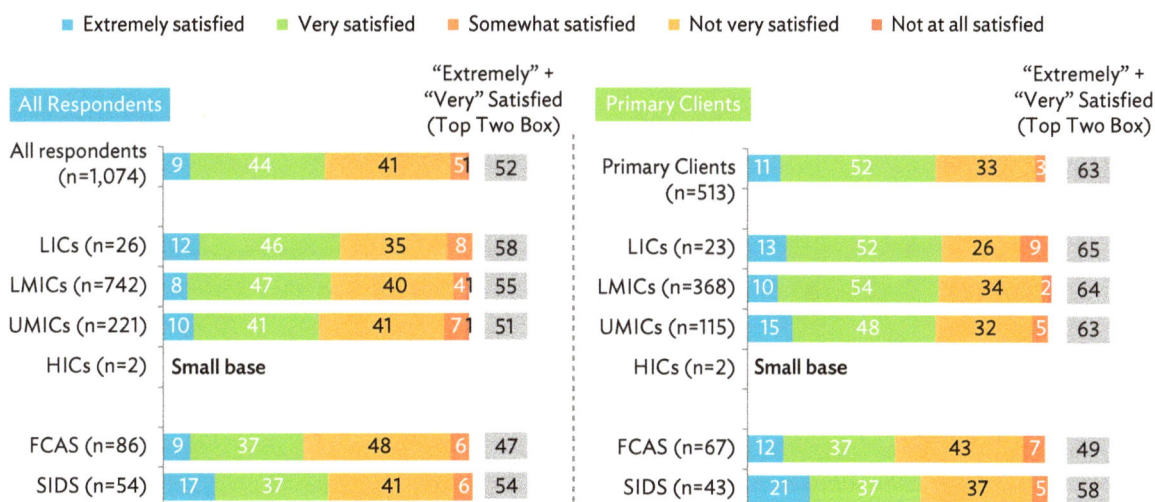

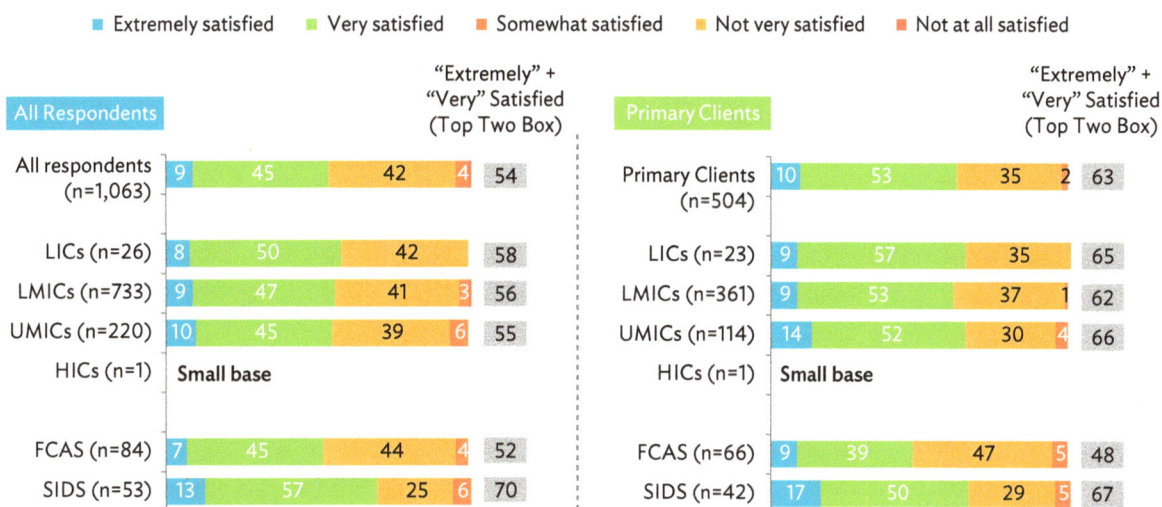

ADB = Asian Development Bank, FCAS = fragile and conflict-affected state, HIC = high-income country, LIC = low-income country, LMIC = lower middle-income country, n = number of respondents, SIDS = small island developing state, UMIC = upper middle-income country.

Note: Survey base – entities familiar with ADB. Small base: n<5.

Source: Asian Development Bank Client Perceptions Survey 2020.

Figure 41: ADB's Collaboration with Development Partners, All Respondents
(%)

■ Extremely satisfied ■ Very satisfied ■ Somewhat satisfied ■ Not very satisfied ■ Not at all satisfied

All Respondents		"Extremely" + "Very" Satisfied (Top Two Box)
All respondents (n=1,063)	9 / 45 / 42 / 4	54
LICs (n=26)	8 / 50 / 42	58
LMICs (n=733)	9 / 47 / 41 / 3	56
UMICs (n=220)	10 / 45 / 39 / 6	55
HICs (n=1)	Small base	
FCAS (n=84)	7 / 45 / 44 / 4	52
SIDS (n=53)	13 / 57 / 25 / 6	70

Primary Clients		"Extremely" + "Very" Satisfied (Top Two Box)
Primary Clients (n=504)	10 / 53 / 35 / 2	63
LICs (n=23)	9 / 57 / 35	65
LMICs (n=361)	9 / 53 / 37 / 1	62
UMICs (n=114)	14 / 52 / 30 / 4	66
HICs (n=1)	Small base	
FCAS (n=66)	9 / 39 / 47 / 5	48
SIDS (n=42)	17 / 50 / 29 / 5	67

ADB = Asian Development Bank, FCAS = fragile and conflict-affected state, HIC = high-income country LIC = low-income country, LMIC = lower middle-income country, n = number of respondents, SIDS = small island developing state, UMIC = upper middle-income country.

Note: Survey base – entities familiar with ADB. Small base: n<5.

Source: Asian Development Bank Client Perceptions Survey 2020.

ADB's COVID-19 Response: Primary Clients

Familiarity

Familiarity with ADB's COVID-19 response is relatively high among Primary Clients (63% claim that they are "very" or "moderately" familiar), as shown in Figure 42.

Among the various country income groups, Primary Clients in LICs are the most familiar with ADB's COVID-19 response in their respective countries (70% are "very" or "moderately" familiar), and those in UMICs, the least familiar (54%).

The level of familiarity stands at 71% among Primary Clients in SIDS, versus 62% among Primary Clients in FCAS.

Results Achieved by ADB in Addressing COVID-19

Figure 43 shows that among Primary Clients that have seen interim results from ADB's response to COVID-19 in their country, the vast majority in all income groups agree that ADB support had some impact.

When country income groups are considered, between 79% and 84% of Primary Clients rate the results and impact of ADB's COVID-19 support "excellent" or "good."

Primary Clients in FCAS give a low rating (68%) to the results achieved by ADB's COVID-19 response in their country, versus a rating of 79% from Primary Clients in SIDS.

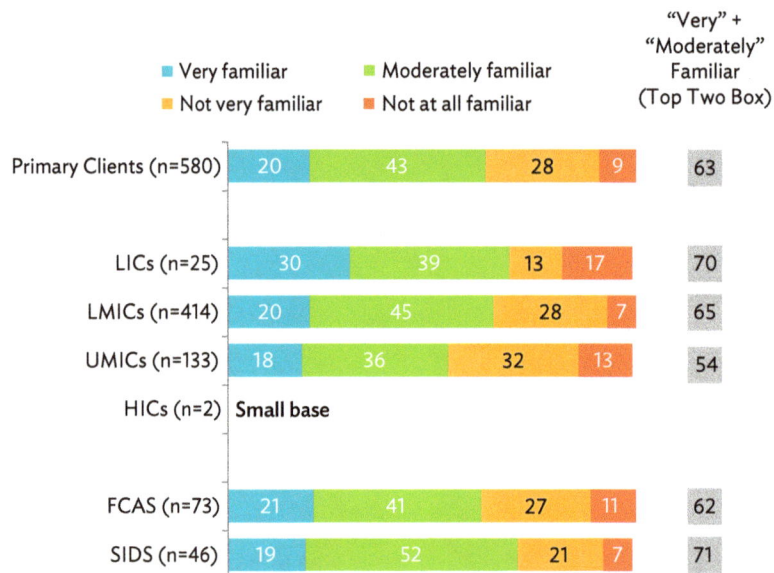

Figure 42: Familiarity with ADB's COVID-19 Response, Primary Clients
(%)

	Very familiar	Moderately familiar	Not very familiar	Not at all familiar	"Very" + "Moderately" Familiar (Top Two Box)
Primary Clients (n=580)	20	43	28	9	63
LICs (n=25)	30	39	13	17	70
LMICs (n=414)	20	45	28	7	65
UMICs (n=133)	18	36	32	13	54
HICs (n=2)	Small base				
FCAS (n=73)	21	41	27	11	62
SIDS (n=46)	19	52	21	7	71

ADB = Asian Development Bank, COVID-19 = coronavirus disease, FCAS = fragile and conflict-affected state, HIC = high-income country, LIC = low-income country, LMIC = lower middle-income country, n = number of respondents, SIDS = small island developing state, UMIC = upper middle-income country.
Note: Survey base – Primary Clients familiar with ADB. Small base: n<5.
Source: Asian Development Bank Client Perceptions Survey 2020.

Figure 43: Results Achieved by ADB in Addressing COVID-19, Primary Clients
(%)

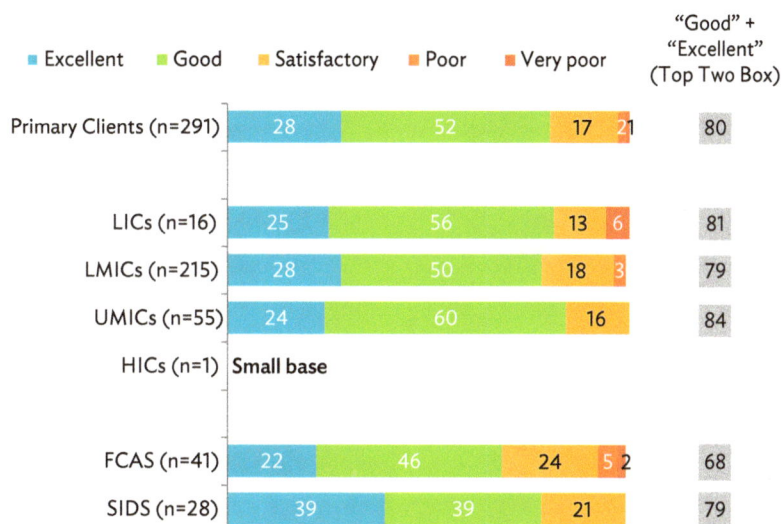

	Excellent	Good	Satisfactory	Poor	Very poor	"Good" + "Excellent" (Top Two Box)
Primary Clients (n=291)	28	52	17	2	1	80
LICs (n=16)	25	56	13		6	81
LMICs (n=215)	28	50	18		3	79
UMICs (n=55)	24	60	16			84
HICs (n=1)	Small base					
FCAS (n=41)	22	46	24	5	2	68
SIDS (n=28)	39	39	21			79

ADB = Asian Development Bank, COVID-19 = coronavirus disease, FCAS = fragile and conflict-affected state, HIC = high-income country LIC = low-income country, LMIC = lower middle-income country, n = number of respondents, SIDS = small island developing state, UMIC = upper middle-income country.

Note: Survey base – Primary Clients familiar with ADB and "very"/"moderately" familiar with ADB's COVID-19 response in their country. Excluded here are those saying that there is as yet "no observed response." Small base: n<5.

Source: Asian Development Bank Client Perceptions Survey 2020.

ADB's Performance in Minimizing Adverse Effects of COVID-19

ADB's performance gets a positive rating overall from Primary Clients, but there are differences between income groups. Primary Clients in LICs and FCAS are less likely than those in UMICs and SIDS to give a positive rating, as can be seen in Figure 44.

Figure 44: ADB's Performance in Minimizing Adverse Effects of COVID-19, Primary Clients (%)

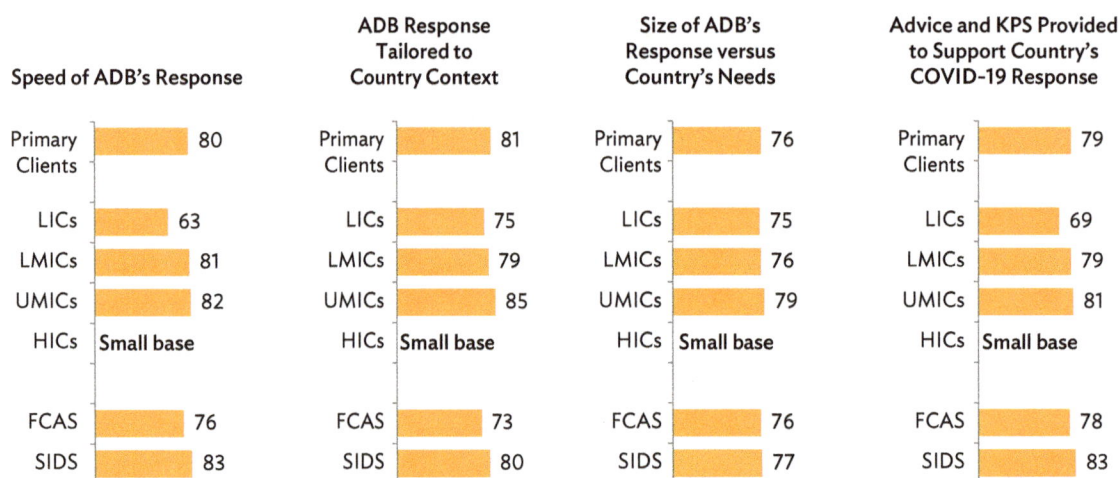

Speed of ADB's Response

Primary Clients	80
LICs	63
LMICs	81
UMICs	82
HICs	Small base
FCAS	76
SIDS	83

ADB Response Tailored to Country Context

Primary Clients	81
LICs	75
LMICs	79
UMICs	85
HICs	Small base
FCAS	73
SIDS	80

Size of ADB's Response versus Country's Needs

Primary Clients	76
LICs	75
LMICs	76
UMICs	79
HICs	Small base
FCAS	76
SIDS	77

Advice and KPS Provided to Support Country's COVID-19 Response

Primary Clients	79
LICs	69
LMICs	79
UMICs	81
HICs	Small base
FCAS	78
SIDS	83

ADB = Asian Development Bank, COVID-19 = coronavirus disease, FCAS = fragile and conflict-affected state, HIC = high-income country LIC = low-income country, LMIC = lower middle-income country, SIDS = small island developing state, UMIC = upper middle-income country.

Note: Survey base – entities familiar with ADB and with ADB's COVID-19 response in their country. Primary Clients = 318 (LICs = 16, LMICs = 234, UMICs = 62, HICs = 1, FCAS = 41, SIDS = 30). Small base: n<5.

Source: Asian Development Bank Client Perceptions Survey 2020.

11 Comparison of 2020 Survey Results with Previous Perception Survey Results

Comparison with the 2012 Client Perceptions Survey

The results are not strictly comparable because of differences in question formulation, response scales, and context. The performance areas discussed below are relatively comparable.

Key Area that Stayed High

Overall image of ADB. Clients see ADB as "trustworthy" and "reliable." Ratings in regard to both remained consistent and high.

Key Areas of Improvement

ADB's performance in some priority areas. Clients perceive improvements in ADB performance, particularly in the following priority areas:

- supporting health care;
- improving education;
- promoting gender equality; and
- promoting environmental sustainability.

Key Area of Decline

ADB's development effectiveness. This declined to 75% in 2020 from 88% in 2012. Clients evidently expect ADB to do better in helping their countries achieve development goals and results.

Key Area that Stayed Low

ADB's collaboration with development partners. This remained relatively low and declined somewhat (63% in 2020 vs. 69% in 2012), showing that clients would like to see enhanced coordination, collaboration, and synergy building among development partners.

CRF Results Framework Indicator Trend, 2020 vs. 2019

The CRF Results Framework Indicator "usefulness of ADB's knowledge products, services, and events" rose in 2020, compared with 2019, among all respondents (3.96 vs. 3.89).

The rise in this CRF indicator was driven mostly by the growing perception among all respondents that ADB KPS are useful in developing learning materials, and in designing and implementing policies and programs, as shown in Figure 45.

This CRF indicator was also significantly higher among Primary Clients in 2020 versus all respondents in 2019. The upswing was mostly due to a higher rating for the usefulness of ADB KPS in implementing policies and programs and in developing learning materials.

Figure 45: Trend in Usefulness of ADB KPS, 2020 vs. 2019

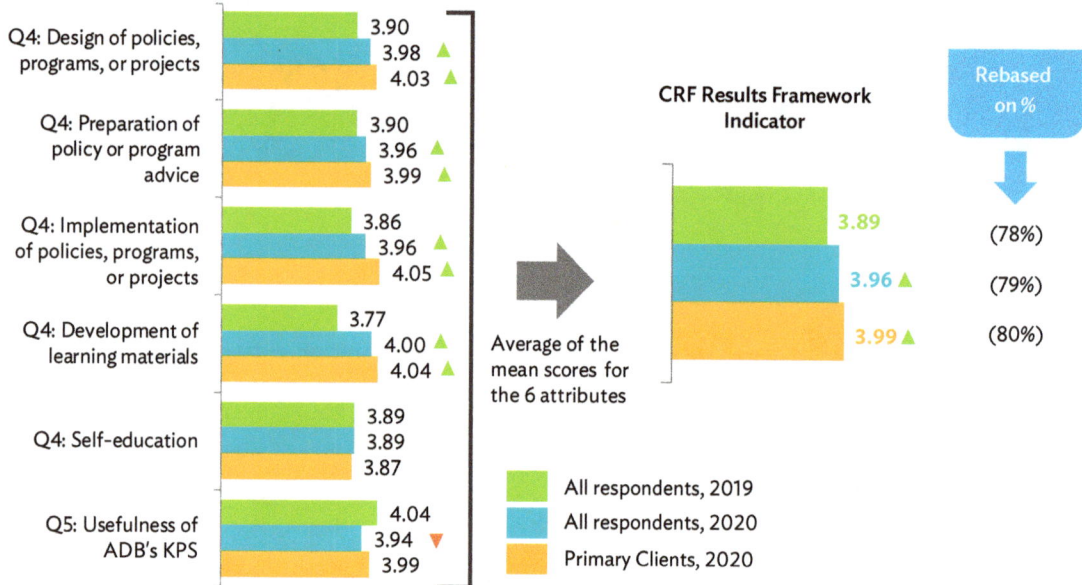

	Score
Q4: Design of policies, programs, or projects	3.90
	3.98 ▲
	4.03 ▲
Q4: Preparation of policy or program advice	3.90
	3.96 ▲
	3.99 ▲
Q4: Implementation of policies, programs, or projects	3.86
	3.96 ▲
	4.05 ▲
Q4: Development of learning materials	3.77
	4.00 ▲
	4.04 ▲
Q4: Self-education	3.89
	3.89
	3.87
Q5: Usefulness of ADB's KPS	4.04
	3.94 ▼
	3.99

Average of the mean scores for the 6 attributes

CRF Results Framework Indicator

Rebased on %

3.89 (78%)
3.96 ▲ (79%)
3.99 ▲ (80%)

- All respondents, 2019
- All respondents, 2020
- Primary Clients, 2020

ADB = Asian Development Bank, CRF = Corporate Results Framework, KPS = knowledge products and services.

Note: Survey base – entities familiar with ADB. Statistically significant. Statistically significant difference: higher ▲ / lower ▼ at 95% confidence level vs. all respondents (2019).

Source: Asian Development Bank Client Perceptions Survey 2020.

12 | Recommendations

Keep ADB knowledge products, services, and events highly relevant and useful

Webinars, seminars, workshops, and conferences are used efficiently by ADB clients. ADB should continue to leverage and develop these products and services as they contribute to building high overall satisfaction with ADB KPS among clients.

Capacity building / Training courses are widely used by Primary Clients and deemed highly useful when used. There is potential for further increasing the use of these products/training as they are very specific to ADB. The main subjects to push forward would be training/support related to policies, programs, and projects (particularly their design and implementation), as well as the knowledge needed to develop learning materials.

Expand the reach of other products to improve relevance and broaden the range of knowledge provided

Books, studies, reports, and working papers, despite being seen as very useful, are used by only half of Primary Clients, leaving room to further increase their use.

The other ADB KPS are also considered highly useful, but they are used by less than half of Primary Clients. To increase product reach, more clients should be encouraged to use these KPS and the usefulness of the products in clients' work should be made evident.

Heighten clients' satisfaction with ADB's responsiveness, development effectiveness, and collaboration with development partners to avoid negative impact and strengthen trust

Inadequate responsiveness and excessive bureaucracy (cf. open-ended question in section 7, Figure 27) are concerns raised by clients to explain some of the negative overall satisfaction ratings of ADB's responsiveness. The context of, and reasons behind, these concerns are worth identifying, to show ADB's willingness to adapt to meet client expectations.

In addition, ADB's development effectiveness is perceived to have declined to 75% in 2020 from 88% in 2012. Although the development context has dramatically changed and development challenges are now much more complex, this perception among DMCs is worthwhile investigating further, to ensure that ADB's efforts keep pace with the evolving development needs of its DMC members.

ADB's collaboration with development partners is rated relatively low, with only 63% of Primary Clients being "extremely" or "very" satisfied. Given the increasingly challenging development context and scarce resources, clients depend highly on close coordination and enhanced collaboration among development partners.

Demonstrating ADB's responsiveness, development effectiveness and collaboration with development partners is also important, in order to avoid any negative effects on overall satisfaction with ADB support at the country level, and to enhance development impact.

Give extra attention to the private sector: make ADB KPS more relevant by customizing knowledge provision, enhancing reach and familiarity to build awareness, and further mobilizing resources for private sector development

Overall, private sector clients are

- less likely to be familiar with ADB KPS;
- less satisfied with the usefulness of these KPS, and with ADB's development effectiveness and responsiveness; and
- less satisfied with ADB's collaboration with development partners.

A similar pattern is observed when it comes to familiarity and satisfaction with ADBI knowledge products and services among private sector clients.

To strengthen awareness of ADB's KPS and of the type of support that ADB can provide to clients in the private sector, ADB can

- develop materials specifically suited to clients' needs;
- showcase the broad range of ADB knowledge products available; and
- give clients stronger guidance in using the new knowledge efficiently in their work.

Moreover, there is room to leverage the successful use of ADB KPS among government organizations and to identify how these KPS can also be effectively applied in the private sector, e.g., by presenting case studies and examples of best practices in training.

Promote the use of ADBI e-learning courses and self-education materials

ADBI KPS are seen as relevant to the main work activities and tasks of the respondents, particularly the design and implementation of new policies, programs, or projects.

Self-education is also regarded by respondents as a relatively important activity in their work, highlighting the potential for ADBI assistance in learning and knowledge development. However, ADBI KPS are deemed slightly less relevant to this task.

Demonstrating the range of ADBI products that can help clients develop and enrich their knowledge will address this perception.

Increase client familiarity with ADB's evaluation KPS and encourage their use

The level of familiarity with these products and services is relatively low among ADB clients: only a third of clients surveyed say they are "very" or "moderately" familiar with ADB's evaluation KPS.

But among clients familiar with these products and services, the vast majority find ADB's evaluation KPS "extremely," "very," or "somewhat" useful. This suggests that there is potential for increasing their effective use by

- building greater awareness of ADB's evaluation KPS;
- showcasing the range of products available to ADB clients; and
- targeting client needs in order to help increase the perceived relevance of these evaluation products and services.

Appendix 1: Survey Methodology

Sampling and Country Samples

The respondents were identified from the client database of the Asian Development Bank (ADB). No quotas or weighting was applied at the country or regional level.

The end-sample totaled 1,436, including 582 Primary Clients—close to the number of Primary Clients in the 2012 client survey (625).

In the completed sample, the split by country was generally representative of the size of ADB borrowers, except for the Philippines, which was overrepresented in the Southeast Asia subregion.

To determine whether this overrepresented sample for the Philippines added a potential bias to the regional results, further analysis was performed. The results of the main indicators for Southeast Asia were compared between the following samples:

- Southeast Asia with 100% of the Philippine sample;
- Southeast Asia with 50% of the Philippine sample;
- Southeast Asia with 30% of the Philippine sample; and
- Southeast Asia with 0% of the Philippine sample.

This analysis showed that weighting down the Philippine sample to 30% of its current size would not affect the regional results significantly (the differences were between +1 and +5 percentage points overall). However, this potential impact should be considered when results at the regional level are read.

Moreover, the total impact would be only between 0 and 1 percentage point.

Geographic Scope

Subregions

The countries where the clients surveyed work were grouped into subregions, as defined by ADB, to reflect the ADB regional grouping of countries. Grouping countries by regions allowed comparisons of the performance of ADB and key indicators to be made between regions.

Coverage, by Subregion

A total of 1,216 respondents took part in the main survey, and 220 respondents participated in a separate short ADBI survey (see page 5 of this report for details).

Central and West Asia   Afghanistan, Armenia, Azerbaijan, Georgia, Kazakhstan, Kyrgyz Republic, Pakistan, Tajikistan, Turkmenistan, Uzbekistan
South Asia   Bangladesh, Bhutan, India, Maldives, Nepal, Sri Lanka
East Asia   People's Republic of China, Mongolia
Southeast Asia   Cambodia, Indonesia, Lao People's Democratic Republic, Myanmar, Philippines, Thailand, Timor-Leste, Viet Nam
Pacific   Cook Islands, Fiji, Kiribati, Marshall Islands, Federated States of Micronesia, Nauru, Niue, Palau, Papua New Guinea, Samoa, Solomon Islands, Tonga, Tuvalu, Vanuatu
Other   All other countries

Fieldwork

The fieldwork took place from 18 December 2020 to 29 January 2021. It involved the following steps:

- **18–24 December 2020: Soft launch.** Invitations were sent to ~1,000 respondents (10%–15% of all respondents). Only English-speaking respondents took part in the soft launch, which was done to find out if the survey needed to be adjusted or revised further. Soft launch interviews/responses are part of the final sample.

- **24 December 2020–29 January 2021: Full launch.** After the soft launch and some survey adjustments, the fieldwork was fully launched. invitations were sent to all the respondents in the database (those who had not yet been invited).

The fieldwork was monitored daily, and detailed checks of interim data were done during the fieldwork (at 10%, 40%, 50%, and 80% of sample completion) to ensure data quality and consistency.

After the fieldwork, final data quality checks were performed. No weighting was applied to the data, and this report presents unweighted results/data.

Overview of the Online Survey Methodology

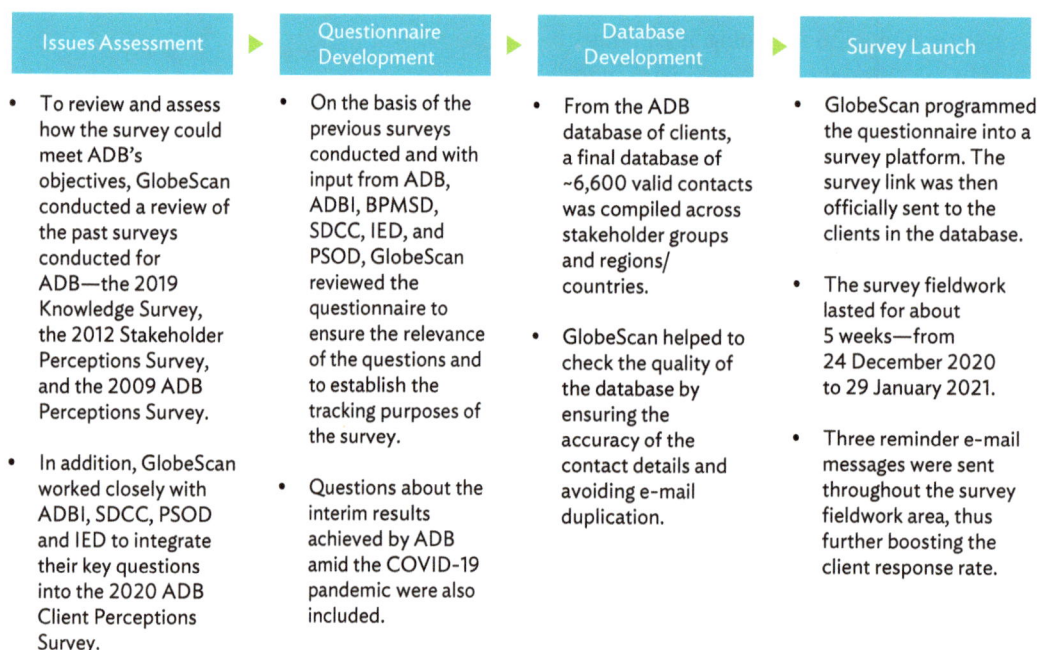

Issues Assessment	Questionnaire Development	Database Development	Survey Launch
• To review and assess how the survey could meet ADB's objectives, GlobeScan conducted a review of the past surveys conducted for ADB—the 2019 Knowledge Survey, the 2012 Stakeholder Perceptions Survey, and the 2009 ADB Perceptions Survey. • In addition, GlobeScan worked closely with ADBI, SDCC, PSOD and IED to integrate their key questions into the 2020 ADB Client Perceptions Survey.	• On the basis of the previous surveys conducted and with input from ADB, ADBI, BPMSD, SDCC, IED, and PSOD, GlobeScan reviewed the questionnaire to ensure the relevance of the questions and to establish the tracking purposes of the survey. • Questions about the interim results achieved by ADB amid the COVID-19 pandemic were also included.	• From the ADB database of clients, a final database of ~6,600 valid contacts was compiled across stakeholder groups and regions/countries. • GlobeScan helped to check the quality of the database by ensuring the accuracy of the contact details and avoiding e-mail duplication.	• GlobeScan programmed the questionnaire into a survey platform. The survey link was then officially sent to the clients in the database. • The survey fieldwork lasted for about 5 weeks—from 24 December 2020 to 29 January 2021. • Three reminder e-mail messages were sent throughout the survey fieldwork area, thus further boosting the client response rate.

ADB = Asian Development Bank, ADBI = Asian Development Bank Institute, BPMSD = Budget, Personnel, and Management Systems Department, COVID-19 = coronavirus disease, IED = Independent Evaluation Department, PSOD = Private Sector Operations Department.

Source: Asian Development Bank Client Perceptions Survey 2020.

Appendix 2: Survey Questionnaire

GlobeScan Incorporated	
Survey:	2020 ADB Client Perceptions Survey
Version:	Master Questionnaire (English)
Date:	23 December, 2020

Sections

1. Screening Questions
2   a. Overall Image of ADB
    b. Overall Perceptions of ADB Knowledge Products and Services
3   Overall Perceptions of ADBI Products, Services and Events
4   Evaluation Knowledge
5   Development Effectiveness
6   Organizational Effectiveness
7   ADB's Technical Assistance Provided to DMCs
8   Impact of COVID-19 and ADB Support
9   Demographics

Programming Notes:

- All programming instructions are in bold, blue, Italic in the questionnaire
- Section headings and question numbers not to be shown in programmed questionnaire
- All questions mandatory unless otherwise stated
- Program in English
- [SA]= Single answer
- [MA]=Multiple answer

Programming: Error Messages

English
An error has occurred on this page. Please fix this error and try again.
A response is required.

Survey Objectives (Do Not Show):

- To keep a pulse on the needs of ADB's sovereign and non-sovereign developing member country (DMC) clients and understand whether ADB is meeting
these needs.
- To generate the corporate results framework (CRF) indicator values:

CRF Results Framework Indicator

- Usefulness of ADB knowledge products (Indicator compiled based on Q4 & Q5)

CRF Tracking Indicators

- Clients satisfied with ADB's development effectiveness (Q15)
- Clients satisfied with ADB's responsiveness (Q17)
- Stakeholders satisfied with ADB's collaboration with development partners (Q19)

Introduction

Welcome to ADB Client Perceptions Survey. Thank you for participating. The survey will take approximately 15 minutes to complete.

The purpose of this survey is to understand the needs of ADB's developing member country clients and understand whether ADB is meeting these needs.

You are encouraged to provide an honest and critical view of ADB's performance and areas of engagement.

Please be assured that your responses to the survey will remain strictly confidential and used only for statistical purposes. To ensure confidentiality, the results of the survey will be compiled and analyzed by an independent research consultancy firm (GlobeScan).

Please read each question carefully before responding. Answer by selecting the response that most closely represents your point of view. Your responses will be tremendously appreciated. Thank you!

Please click "Next" to begin the survey.

If you have any technical questions about the survey, please contact Ellen Tops at etops.consultant@adb.org;
for other questions, please contact Angie Cortez at acortez@adb.org; or you can e-mail the survey team at adbclientsurvey@adb.org.

Section 1: Screening Questions

To begin, we would like to ask a few questions to learn more about you and how much you know about the Asian Development Bank (ADB).

Ask All

S1. Please select the language from the list below in which you would like to complete the survey:

1	English
2	Chinese (Simplified Mandarin)
3	Bahasa
4	Russian

Ask All

S2a. How knowledgeable would you say you are about the Asian Development Bank and its activities? *[SA]*

1	Very knowledgeable
2	Somewhat knowledgeable
3	Not too knowledgeable
4	Not knowledgeable at all *[See instruction after S2b]*

Ask All

S2b. How knowledgeable would you say you are about the Asian Development Bank Institute (ADBI) and its activities? *[SA]*

1	Very knowledgeable
2	Somewhat knowledgeable
3	Not too knowledgeable
4	Not knowledgeable at all

TERMINATE interview if: "Not knowledgeable at all" of ADB in S2a (code 4), and 'Not too knowledgeable' or "Not knowledgeable at all" of ADBI (code 3 or 4 in S2b)

If "Not knowledgeable at all" of ADB (code 4 in S2a) AND knowledgeable of ADBI (codes 1 or 2 in S2b) only ask Section 1, Section 3, and Section 9 to these respondents.

FOR the separate ADBI database: ask Section 1, Section 3 and Section 9 only to these respondents.

S3a & S3b – REMOVED

Ask All

S4. From the following list, please choose the country where you currently work. **[SA]**

Central and West Asia	1	Afghanistan
	2	Armenia
	3	Azerbaijan
	4	Georgia
	5	Kazakhstan
	6	Kyrgyz Republic
	7	Pakistan
	8	Tajikistan
	9	Turkmenistan
	10	Uzbekistan
East Asia	11	Mongolia
	12	People's Republic of China
Pacific	13	Cook Islands
	14	Fiji
	15	Kiribati
	16	Marshall Islands
	17	Federated States of Micronesia
	18	Nauru
	19	Niue
	20	Palau
	21	Papua New Guinea
	22	Samoa
	23	Solomon Islands
	24	Tonga
	25	Tuvalu
	26	Vanuatu
South Asia	27	Bangladesh
	28	Bhutan
	29	India
	30	Maldives
	31	Nepal
	32	Sri Lanka
Southeast Asia	33	Cambodia
	34	Indonesia
	35	Lao People's Democratic Republic
	36	Myanmar
	37	Philippines
	38	Thailand
	39	Timor-Leste
	40	Viet Nam
Other	41	Other

Ask All

S5. From the list below, please select the organization that best describes where you work. **[SA]**

1	Government 1 (Prime Minister's/President's office, Ministries of Finance, Economy, Development, Planning, Parliament/Legislature)
2	Government 2 (Ministries/Departments, i.e., Transport, Energy, Agriculture, Health, Education, Industry and Trade, etc.)
3	Government 3 (regional, provincial, and municipal)
4	Civil society organization (i.e., nongovernment organization, charity, not-for-profit)
5	Private/Business sector
6	Media
7	University, think tank, academia
8	Others (Please specify):

Section 2a: Overall Image of ADB

Ask All, except those "Not at all knowledgeable" of ADB (code 4 in S2a)

Q1a. To what extent do you agree or disagree that the following statements accurately describe the Asian Development Bank? **[MA]**

	Strongly disagree	Disagree	Neither agree, nor disagree	Agree	Strongly agree
Knowledgeable	1	2	3	4	5
Solution Oriented	1	2	3	4	5
Trustworthy	1	2	3	4	5
Transparent	1	2	3	4	5
Innovative	1	2	3	4	5
Collaborative	1	2	3	4	5
Forward-looking	1	2	3	4	5
Agile	1	2	3	4	5
Reliable	1	2	3	4	5
Efficient	1	2	3	4	5

Section 2b: Overall Perceptions of ADB Knowledge Products and Services

Show the introduction text below on a separate screen before Q1b

ADB is strengthening its role as a knowledge provider and works closely with its developing member countries to identify their needs, and to produce the most relevant knowledge products, services, and events.

Ask All, except those "Not at all knowledgeable" of ADB (code 4 in S2a)

Q1b. ADB distributes knowledge-rich content and activities that enable, facilitate, or support decisions or actions by intended users.

How familiar are you with ADB knowledge products and services such as flagship publications, technical studies, policy briefs, op-eds, capacity building/ training, etc.? *[SA]*

Not Familiar at all	Not very Familiar	Moderately Familiar	Very Familiar
1	2	3	4

Ask those familiar of ADB Knowledge Products and Services: codes 2, 3, or 4 in Q1b

If code 1 selected in Q1b, go to Q10a

Q2. Which of the following ADB knowledge products, services, and/or events have you used for your work? Please select all the knowledge products, services, and/or events you have used in the past, even if only once. *[MA]*

1	a. Books/ technical studies/ reports/ working papers (e.g., Asian Development Outlook, Sustainability Report, Development Effectiveness Review, etc.)
2	b. Short reports (policy briefs, blogs, op-eds, etc.)
3	c. Multimedia (podcasts, videos, infographics, PowerPoint presentations, etc.)
4	d. Policy dialogue and related activities
5	e. Capacity building/ Training
5	f. Processes, project management and technical capacity development
6	g. Webinars, seminars, workshops, and conferences
7	h. None of these (Skip to Q10a)

Ask for each product/service used in the past: each code selected in Q2.

If no code selected in Q2, go to Q10a.

Q3. Please rate on a scale of 1 to 5 (1 being "not at all useful" and 5 being "extremely useful") the usefulness of the following ADB's knowledge products, services, and events: *[SA]*

	Not at all useful	Not very useful	Somewhat useful	Very useful	Extremely useful
a. Books/ technical studies/ reports/ working papers (e.g., Asian Development Outlook, Sustainability Report, etc.)	1	2	3	4	5
b. Short reports (policy briefs, blogs, op-eds, etc.)	1	2	3	4	5
c. Multimedia (podcasts, videos, infographics, presentations, etc.)	1	2	3	4	5
d. Policy dialogue and related activities	1	2	3	4	5
e. Capacity building/ Training	1	2	3	4	5
f. Processes, project management and technical capacity development	1	2	3	4	5
g. Webinars, Seminars, workshops, and conferences	1	2	3	4	5

Ask Q4 if at least one code was selected in Q2

If no code selected in Q2, go to Q10a

Q4. Please rate the usefulness of ADB's knowledge products, services, and events (based on a 5-point scale with 1 being lowest and 5 being highest), in terms of: *[SA]*

	Not at all Useful	Not very useful	Somewhat Useful	Very Useful	Extremely Useful	Don't Know/ Not Applicable
Preparing policy or program advice	1	2	3	4	5	6
Designing policy, programs or projects	1	2	3	4	5	6
Implementing policy, programs or projects	1	2	3	4	5	6
Developing learning materials	1	2	3	4	5	6
Self-education	1	2	3	4	5	6

Ask Q5 if at least one code was selected in Q2

If no code selected in Q2, go to Q10a

Q5. Overall, please rate the usefulness of ADB's knowledge products, services, and events (based on a 5-point scale with 1 being lowest and 5 being highest). *[SA]*

	Not at all useful	Not very useful	Somewhat useful	Very useful	Extremely useful
Overall usefulness of ADB knowledge products, services, and events	1	2	3	4	5

Ask Q6 if at least one code was selected in Q2

If no code selected in Q2, go to Q10a

Q6. What is/are the reason(s) for your rating on overall usefulness of ADB Knowledge Products and Services? *[Open-Ended]*

Please indicate all the reasons for which you gave this rating.

Ask Q7 if at least one code was selected in Q2

If no code selected in Q2, go to Q10a

Q7. Overall, how would you rate the timeliness of the delivery of ADB knowledge products and services to you? *[SA]*

	Very poor	Poor	Satisfactory	Good	Excellent
Timeliness of the delivery of ADB knowledge products and services to you	1	2	3	4	5

Ask Q8 if at least one code was selected in Q2

If no code selected in Q2, go to Q10a

Q8. Were you able to apply any of the information and ideas contained in the ADB knowledge products, services, or events? *[SA]*

1	Yes *[Go to Q9a]*
2	No *[Go to Q10a]*

Q9a. Were there any benefits from applying those information and ideas? *[SA]*

By benefits we mean, for example, how ADB's policy dialogue contributed to your institutional reform, policy changes, or how much you benefited from i t.

1	Yes [*Go to Q9b*]
2	No [*Go to Q10a*]

Ask those who select "Yes" in Q9a (code 1)

Programmer: Monitor ranking of the benefits selected; the respondent can select 0, 1, 2, or 3 benefits.

Q9b. Which were the benefits from the application of information and ideas contained in the ADB knowledge products, services, or events?

Please indicate up to 3 benefits that come to your mind, in order of importance. *[SA]*

		Ranking (3 most important benefits)
1	Data and information were used in policy, reports, and articles	
2	Better decision-making	
3	Clearer understanding of policy issues and implications	
4	Empowered and motivated staff	
5	Helped in formulating policies	
6	Helped in writing reports, speeches	
7	Improved environmental policy and assessment	
8	Improved project designing and implementation	
9	Increased work efficiency	
10	Gained knowledge on implementing climate change related actions	
11	Gained knowledge on procurement and monitoring tools	
12	Learned new innovation ideas	
13	Learned policy formulation and advice	
14	Learned how to prepare contracts	
15	Accessed quality researches	
16	Learned about socio-economic development in rural areas	
17	Gained knowledge on trade and investment	
18	Increased knowledge from capacity building and training courses	
19	Others (Please specify):	

Ask All, except those "Not at all knowledgeable" of ADB (code 4 in S2a)

Q10a. Please rate the quality of the knowledge materials disseminated by the following entities: *[SA]*

	Very poor	Poor	Satisfactory	Good	Very good	Don't know
the government of [name of country]	1	2	3	4	5	6
the United Nations Development Programme (UNDP)	1	2	3	4	5	6
the World Bank	1	2	3	4	5	6
the Asian Development Bank (ADB)	1	2	3	4	5	6
the International Monetary Fund (IMF)	1	2	3	4	5	6

Ask All, except those "Not at all knowledgeable" of ADB (code 4 in S2a)

Q10b. And which of the following entities is the best in disseminating knowledge in *[insert country from S4]*? The second best? And which one is the third best?

		Rank (1 to 3)
1	the government of *[insert country from S4]*	
2	the United Nations Development Programme (UNDP)	
3	the World Bank	
4	the Asian Development Bank (ADB)	
5	the International Monetary Fund (IMF)	

Q10c & Q10d – REMOVED

Section 3: Overall Perceptions of ADBI Products, Services and Events

Ask Section 3 only to those familiar with ADBI (codes 1 or 2 in S2b), If "Not too knowledgeable" or "Not knowledgeable at all" (code 3 or 4 in S2b), go to Section 4, Q11.

Show the introduction text below on a separate screen before Q1ADBI

The Asian Development Bank Institute (ADBI) helps build capacity, skills, and knowledge related to poverty reduction and other areas that support long-term growth and competitiveness in developing economies in Asia and the Pacific.

Ask those familiar with ADBI (codes 1 or 2 in S2b)

Q1a(ADBI). How familiar are you with ADBI policy dialogues, training programs, e-learning courses and other capacity building products? *[SA]*

Not familiar at all	Not very familiar	Moderately familiar	Very familiar
1	2	3	4

Ask those familiar with ADBI (codes 1 or 2 in S2b)

Q1b(ADBI). How familiar are you with ADBI webinars, blogs, reports, books, journal issues, and other research products?

Not familiar at all	Not very familiar	Moderately familiar	Very familiar
1	2	3	4

Ask those familiar with ADBI (codes 1 or 2 in S2b). If code 4 in S2b, go to Q11)

Q2ADBI. Please rate on a scale of 1 to 5 (1 being "not at all relevant" and 5 being "extremely relevant") how relevant the following ADBI knowledge products, services, and events are for your work? *[SA]*

	Not at all relevant	Not very relevant	Somewhat relevant	Very relevant	Extremely relevant	I'm not familiar with this product/ service
a. Books, reports, journal issues	1	2	3	4	5	6
b. Short publications, such as policy briefs, blogs, articles	1	2	3	4	5	6
c. Research webinars, seminars, workshops, and conferences	1	2	3	4	5	6
d. Policy dialogues	1	2	3	4	5	6
e. Capacity building/ Training events	1	2	3	4	5	6
f. E-learning courses	1	2	3	4	5	6
g. Social media, video or podcasts	1	2	3	4	5	6

Ask if at least one code 3, 4, or 5 was selected in Q2ADBI

If not familiar with all products (code 6 in Q2ADBI for all items a, b, c, d, e, f, g) or not relevant (codes 1, 2 in Q2ADBI), go to Q8ADBI

Q3ADBI. Please rate the relevance of ADBI's knowledge products, services, and events (based on a 5-point scale with 1 being lowest and 5 being highest), in terms of: *[SA]*

	Not at all relevant	Not very relevant	Somewhat relevant	Very relevant	Extremely relevant
Preparing policy or program advice	1	2	3	4	5
Designing policy, programs or projects	1	2	3	4	5
Implementing policy, programs or projects	1	2	3	4	5
Developing learning materials	1	2	3	4	5
Self-education and enrichment	1	2	3	4	5

Ask if at least one code 3, 4 or 5 was selected in Q2ADBI

If not familiar with all products (code 6 in Q2ADBI for all items a, b, c, d, e, f, g) or not relevant (codes 1, 2 in Q2ADBI), go to Q8ADBI

Q4ADBI. Overall, please rate the relevance of ADBI knowledge products, services, and events for your work? *[SA]*

	Not at all relevant	Not very relevant	Somewhat relevant	Very relevant	Extremely relevant
Overall relevance of ADBI knowledge products, services, and events	1	2	3	4	5

Ask if at least one code 3, 4 or 5 was selected in Q2ADBI

If not familiar with all products (code 6 in Q2ADBI for all items a, b, c, d, e, f, g) or not relevant (codes 1, 2 in Q2ADBI), go to Q8ADBI

Q5ADBI. Please indicate to which extent the following actions/ tasks are important in your work. *[SA]*

	Not at all important	Not very important	Somewhat important	Very important	Extremely important	Don't know / Not applicable
Preparing policy or program advice	1	2	3	4	5	6
Designing policy, programs or projects	1	2	3	4	5	6
Implementing policy, programs or projects	1	2	3	4	5	6
Developing learning materials	1	2	3	4	5	6
Self-education and enrichment	1	2	3	4	5	6

Ask if at least one code 3, 4 or 5 was selected in Q2ADBI

If not familiar with all products (code 6 in Q2ADBI for all items a, b, c, d, e, f, g) or not relevant (codes 1, 2 in Q2ADBI), go to Q8ADBI

Q6ADBI. Were there any benefits from the application of information and ideas contained in the ADBI knowledge products or events? *[SA]*

1	Yes [*Go to Q7ADBI*]
2	No [*Go to Q8ADBI*]

Ask those who select "Yes" in Q6ADBI (code 1)

Programmer: Monitor ranking of the benefits selected; the respondent can select 0, 1, 2, or 3 benefits.

Q7ADBI. Which were the benefits from the application of information and ideas contained in the ADBI knowledge products or events?

Please indicate up to 3 benefits that come to your mind, in order of importance. *[SA]*

		Ranking (3 most important benefits)
1	Data and information were used in policy, reports, and articles	
2	Better decision-making	
3	Clearer understanding of policy issues and implications	
4	Empowered and motivated staff	
5	Helped in formulating policies	
6	Helped in writing reports, speeches	
7	Improved project designing and implementation	
8	Increased work efficiency	
9	Gained knowledge on procurement and monitoring tools	
10	Learned new policy ideas	
11	Learned policy formulation and advice	
12	Accessed quality research	
13	Increased knowledge from capacity building and training courses	
14	Others (Please specify):	

Ask those familiar with ADBI (codes 1 or 2 in S2b)

Q8ADBI. Please indicate to which extent you agree or disagree with the following statement:

ADBI is an excellent source of knowledge on development issues *[SA]*

Strongly disagree	Somewhat disagree	Neither agree, nor disagree	Somewhat agree	Strongly agree
1	2	3	4	5

Section 4: Evaluation Knowledge

Ask All

Q11. ADB's Independent Evaluation Department (IED) provides evaluation-related content and activities that inform, enable, facilitate, or support decisions or actions by intended users.

How familiar are you with IED's evaluation knowledge products and services such as evaluation reports, videos, workshops, and seminars, etc.? *[SA]*

Not Familiar at all	Not very Familiar	Moderately Familiar	Very Familiar
1	2	3	4

Ask those familiar with IED (codes 2, 3, or 4 in Q11)

If "Not at all familiar" (code 1 in Q11), go to Q15

Q12. Please indicate if you agree, neither agree nor disagree, or disagree with the following statement: ADB's Independent Evaluation is an important source of learning. *[SA]*

1	Agree
2	Neither agree, nor disagree
3	Disagree

Ask those familiar with IED (codes 2, 3, or 4 in Q11)

If "Not at all familiar"(code 1 in Q11), go to Q15

Q13. Please rate on a scale of 1 to 5 (1 being "not at all useful" and 5 being "extremely useful") the usefulness of the following Evaluation Knowledge outputs or products: *[SA]*

	Not at all useful	Not very useful	Somewhat useful	Very useful	Extremely useful	I'm not familiar with this product
a. Evaluation reports	1	2	3	4	5	6
b. Evaluation recommendations	1	2	3	4	5	6
c. Evaluation lessons	1	2	3	4	5	6
d. Evaluation illustrated (using infographics)	1	2	3	4	5	6
e. Evaluation in brief (2–4 pagers)	1	2	3	4	5	6
f. Evaluation dissemination events Videos	1	2	3	4	5	6
g. Asian Evaluation Week	1	2	3	4	5	6
h. Evaluation workshops and trainings	1	2	3	4	5	6

Ask those familiar with IED (codes 2, 3, or 4 in Q11)

If "Not at all familiar" (code 1 in Q11), go to Q15

Q14. What do you use Evaluation Knowledge for? Please select all that apply. *[MA]*

1	Informing my decisions
2	Informing my work
3	Designing new policies, strategies, programs, projects
4	Deepening my understanding of development issues
5	Promoting change
6	None of these

Section 5: Development Effectiveness

Show the introduction text below on a separate screen before Q15

ADB has been a key partner in the significant transformation of the Asia and the Pacific region and is committed to continue serving the region in the next phase of its development.

Ask All, except those "Not at all knowledgeable" of ADB (code 4 in S2a)

Q15. How effective is ADB in helping your country achieve development results?

Please rate your level of satisfaction with ADB's development effectiveness in your country. *[SA]*

Not at all satisfied	Not very satisfied	Somewhat satisfied	Very satisfied	Extremely satisfied
1	2	3	4	5

Ask All, except those "Not at all knowledgeable" of ADB (code 4 in S2a)

Q16. For each of the following areas, please rate the Asian Development Bank's performance in your country. *[SA by area]*

[ROTATE statements]	Very poor	Poor	Satisfactory	Good	Excellent	DK / NA
a. Fostering regional cooperation and integration	1	2	3	4	5	6
b. Making cities more livable	1	2	3	4	5	6
c. Reducing inequality	1	2	3	4	5	6
d. Promoting environmental sustainability	1	2	3	4	5	6
e. Providing disaster and emergency assistance	1	2	3	4	5	6
f. Improving the infrastructure	1	2	3	4	5	6
g. Supporting health care	1	2	3	4	5	6
h. Improving education and training	1	2	3	4	5	6
i. Promoting rural development and food security	1	2	3	4	5	6
j. Mobilizing resources to develop the private sector	1	2	3	4	5	6
k. Promoting gender equality	1	2	3	4	5	6
l. Strengthening governance and institutional capacity	1	2	3	4	5	6
m. Providing integrated solutions to development challenges	1	2	3	4	5	6
n. Reducing poverty	1	2	3	4	5	6
o. Supporting climate change adaptation and/or mitigation	1	2	3	4	5	6
p. Supporting disaster risk management	1	2	3	4	5	6

Section 6: Organizational Effectiveness

Show the introduction text below on a separate screen before Q17

ADB sustains its efforts and customizes its approach to respond effectively to the Asia and the Pacific region's evolving and diverse needs.

Ask All, except those "Not at all knowledgeable" of ADB (code 4 in S2a)

Q17. How satisfied are you with ADB's responsiveness when it comes to meeting your needs? *[SA]*

Not at all satisfied	Not very satisfied	Somewhat satisfied	Very satisfied	Extremely satisfied
1	2	3	4	5

Ask All, except those "Not at all knowledgeable" of ADB (code 4 in S2a)

Q18. What is/are the reason(s) for your rating on ADB's responsiveness in meeting your needs? *[Open-Ended]*

Please indicate all the reasons for which you gave this rating.

Show the text below on a separate screen before Q19

ADB is strengthening dialogue and collaboration with development partners, including international financial institutions, bilateral development partners, charitable and philanthropic organizations, civil society organizations (CSOs), and the private sector to better assist development efforts in the Asia and the Pacific region.

Ask All, except those "Not at all knowledgeable" of ADB (code 4 in S2a)

Q19. How effective is ADB in its collaboration with its development partners? Please rate your level of satisfaction with ADB's collaboration with various development partners. *[SA]*

Not at all satisfied	Not very satisfied	Somewhat satisfied	Very satisfied	Extremely satisfied
1	2	3	4	5

Q20a - REMOVED

Section 7: ADB's Technical Assistance Provided to DMCs

Ask All, except those "Not at all knowledgeable" of ADB (code 4 in S2a)

Q20b. To what extent do you agree or disagree with the following statements about ADB's technical assistance provided to *[insert country from S4]*. *[SA]*

	Strongly disagree	Disagree	Neither agree, nor disagree	Agree	Strongly agree
ADB's technical assistance operations align well with *[insert country from S4]*'s national development priorities	1	2	3	4	5
ADB's technical assistance operations effectively addresses *[insert country from S4]*'s knowledge needs	1	2	3	4	5
The ADB process for providing technical assistance is efficient	1	2	3	4	5

Section 8: Impact of COVID-19 and ADB support

Ask All, except those "Not at all knowledgeable" of ADB (code 4 in S2a)

Q21. How familiar are you with ADB's COVID-19 response in your country? *[SA]*

Not Familiar at all	Not very Familiar	Moderately Familiar	Very Familiar
1	2	3	4

If "Not at all knowledgeable" of ADB (code 4 in S2a) and/or "Not familiar at all" with ADB's COVID response (code 1 in Q21), skip to Q24

Q22. For each of the following, how would you rate ADB's performance when it comes to meeting your country's development needs to minimize adverse effects of COVID-19? *[SA]*

	Very poor	Poor	Satisfactory	Good	Excellent	No support received during the pandemic
The speed of ADB's response to address COVID-19	1	2	3	4	5	99
ADB tailoring its response to the context of your country	1	2	3	4	5	99
The size of ADB's response versus your country's needs	1	2	3	4	5	99
ADB providing advice, knowledge products, services and events to support your COVID-19 response	1	2	3	4	5	99

If "Not at all knowledgeable" of ADB (code 4 in S2a) and/or "Not familiar at all" with ADB's COVID response (code 1 in Q21), skip to Q24

Q23. What is your view on the impacts of ADB's support to address COVID-19 in your country? Please rate the results achieved by ADB in your country to address COVID-19. *[SA]*

	Very poor	Poor	Satisfactory	Good	Excellent	No observed results yet / Too early
Results achieved by ADB in *[insert country from S4]* to address COVID-19	1	2	3	4	5	99

Section 9: Demographics

Ask All

Q24. What is your gender? *[SA]*

1	Female
2	Male
3	Gender reflected in other ways
4	Prefer not to say

Ask All

Q25. Could you please indicate your age? *[SA]*

1. 18-19
2. 20-24
3. 25-29
4. 30-34
5. 35-39
6. 40-44
7. 45-49
8. 50-54
9. 55-59
10. 60-65
11. 65 and above
12. Prefer not to say

Ask All

Q26. How many years have you been working in a development institution? *[SA]*

1	Less than 5 years
2	5 to 10 years
3	More than 10 years
4	Not applicable

Ask All

Q27. Please select your level of seniority / job grade from the options below. *[SA]*

1	Executive
2	Director / General Manager
3	Manager
4	Officer / Engineer / Surveyor
5	Other

Thank you for participating in this survey.

Please click the Submit button to close this interview.